SUPPORTING WESTMINSTER

THIS BOOK WAS WRITTEN to support the mission of Westminster Theological Seminary, which seeks to train specialists in the Bible to proclaim the whole counsel of God for Christ and his global church. Westminster is committed to the Reformed faith and the Westminster Confession, upholding God's changeless and inerrant word in the midst of a changing world. To learn more about Westminster and to support her mission, visit www.wts.edu/donate. Or contact the Stewardship Office at 215-572-3830.

PRAISE FOR THE CHRIST-LIGHT

"Pierce has often given me good counsel and prayer support. In this book, he presents a fresh and biblical account of Christ's presence in believers, using the biblical metaphor of Christ as a threefold light. I commend it to all who want to know Jesus better."

> — **John M. Frame**, author of *Systematic Theology* and The Theology of Lordship series, former J. D. Trimble Chair of Systematic Theology and Philosophy at Reformed Theological Seminary

"A combination of rich, deep theology, vivid illustration, poetic feeling, and the wonder of the theme of light in Scripture make this book a wonder to read."

> — **Vern S. Poythress**, author of *The Mystery of the Trinity*, *In the Beginning Was the Word*, and *God-Centered Biblical Interpretation*, Distinguished Professor of New Testament, Biblical Interpretation, and Systematic Theology at Westminster Theological Seminary

"This is a remarkable book, a blend of good theology, extensive reflection, poetic insight, and incisive application. It points beyond the messy world of sin and depravity to the glorious transformative process enacted by Christ through his Spirit. It fills a real void."

> — **Robert Letham**, author of *The Holy Trinity*, *Systematic Theology*, and *The Holy Spirit*, Professor of Systematic and Historical Theology, Union School of Theology

"*The Christ-Light* bears all my favorite things: poetry, theology, humility, curiosity, warmth, beauty, and love. This is a book to read alone in holy contemplation, and it's a book to read in community for godly action. It's wonderful."

> — **Karen Swallow Prior**, author of *The Evangelical Imagination: How Stories, Images & Metaphors Created a Culture in Crisis*

THE CHRIST-LIGHT

ALSO BY THE AUTHOR

In Divine Company
Theological English
The Trinity, Language, and Human Behavior
The Speaking Trinity & His Worded World
Finding God in the Ordinary
Struck Down but Not Destroyed
Still, Silent, and Strong
Finding Hope in Hard Things
The Book of Giving
I Am a Human
God of Words
The Great Lie
Christmas Glory
Borrowed Images
word by Word
One with God
Wielding Words
Insider-Outsider

THE CHRIST-LIGHT

Given by God, Glowing in You, Offered for Others

Pierce Taylor Hibbs

Truth Ablaze

Copyright © 2023 Pierce Taylor Hibbs. All rights reserved. Except for brief quotations, no part of this book may be reproduced in any manner without prior written consent from the author. For more information, visit piercetaylorhibbs.com.

ISBN: 979-8-9861067-9-3

Scripture quotations are from the ESV® Bible (The Holy Bible, English Standard Version®), copyright © 2001 by Crossway, a publishing ministry of Good News Publishers. Used by permission. All rights reserved.

Cover art: Albert Bierstadt, *The Rocky Mountains, Lander's Peak*, oil on linen, 1863

CONTENTS

1. A Note about Audience — 1
2. Introduction — 5
3. The God of Light — 13
4. Creatures of Light, Fallen and Redeemed — 21
5. The Light of the World — 49
6. The Light in the World — 57
7. Seeing as a Servant — 67
8. Seeing the Sheep — 73
9. Unveiling the Light with Questions — 79
10. Seeing Light by Telling Stories — 87
11. Unrestricted Forgiveness — 97
12. What Brightening Looks Like — 107
13. Love and Giving — 119
14. Conclusion — 129
15. Appendix 1 — 131
16. Appendix 2 — 135

Endnotes — 141

For the donors of Westminster Theological Seminary. In partnering with us to train specialists in the Bible, you create more light in the world—a light that can only radiate from Christ, who illumines all of us. May we all flock to him.

A Note about Audience

THIS IS A BOOK written for Christians and assumes a great deal about the Christian faith. When read by a different audience, it may be misunderstood. Since I'd like to avoid that, you should know upfront what I'm assuming theologically. You may disagree with me, of course, but you won't fairly understand my message apart from these assumptions.

In this book, I assume . . .

- The authority, truth, sufficiency, and trustworthiness of God's word;

- The fallen state of humanity and our complete depravity (Rom. 3:10–18, 23);

- The mysterious, electing love of God in pursuing rebellious creatures (John 3:16; Rom. 5:7–8, 10; 8:29);

- The identity and new life of people who believe in Christ as Lord (2 Cor. 5:17; Rom. 8:1–8);

- The ultimate expression of love as self-sacrifice or self-giving (John 3:16).

Some readers might wonder, "What about non-Christians? If they don't have the light of Christ in them, how should we engage with them?" I deal with this question in an appendix, but the short answer is that while non-Christians are shown common grace and may display traits we associate with the Christian faith (e.g., kindness, generosity, patience, self-sacrifice), Scripture is clear that apart from Christ, we're dead (Eph. 2:1–3). But our lifeless state doesn't just mean there's no "light" in us (an absence of something); it also means that we're corrupted and corrupting (Rom. 1:28–32). We pollute and destroy both ourselves and others unless we're bound in union to the true, good, redeeming shepherd.

The goal of this book is to help Christians understand what sort of light they have inside them because of Christ's work and how they can look for that light and draw it out in other believers. Engaging with non-believers would require a separate book. In fact, for that I would direct readers to *Insider Outsider: How God Makes Insiders from Outsiders & Helps Us Talk about Our Faith.*

The Christ-Light

God lit a candle in your chest.
The wax is of the very best.
The wick is woven strong, unbreaking,
And the flame is of the Spirit's making.

INTRODUCTION

When you met Jesus Christ, when you embraced him and he embraced you, God lit a candle in your chest. That was a beautiful moment, wasn't it? A moment of hope and healing, overwhelming joy and gratitude. For most of us it was a moment of profound direction, setting our feet on a path winding into a horizon of ceaseless communion with the one who fully knows and fiercely loves us.

And yet, in another sense he lit that candle a long time ago—before there were trees or birds or beasts; before there were skies or seas; before there was light itself in the wild world; when it was just a happy and holy meeting of Father, Son, and Spirit, deep as a million summer suns. There, with himself—the best of company—God lit a candle in your chest. He did it in his eternal counsel, choosing you in Christ before the foundation of the world (Eph. 1:4). Paul writes, "For those whom he foreknew he also predestined to be conformed to the image of his Son, in order that he might be the firstborn among many brothers" (Rom. 8:29). God *foreknew* you. He *foreknew* me. And so even before the beginning of anything, he lit a candle in your chest and mine. And he did it with his Son at heart—so that the light of Christ would be preeminent (Col. 1:18), the God-candle drawing all lesser lights to himself—a congregation of illumination.

But what is this candle? It's something beautiful, something crafted and set burning by God himself, of course, but it's *not* what theologians call *the image of God*, though we'll talk about that.[1] It's what I'm going to call *the Christ-light*. Look at how Paul describes it in Ephesians 5:8–14.

> For at one time you were darkness, but now you are light in the Lord. Walk as children of light (for the fruit of light is found in all that is good and right and true), and try to discern what is pleasing to the Lord. Take no part in the unfruitful works of darkness, but instead expose them. For it is shameful even to speak of the things that they do in secret. But when anything is exposed by the light, it becomes visible, for anything that becomes visible is light. Therefore it says, "Awake, O sleeper, and arise from the dead, and Christ will shine on you."

Apart from Christ, we *were* darkness—not just *in* darkness or *covered by* darkness. But in Christ we *are* light. Do you see the grand reversal, the death-to-life transition? That's an amazing truth, a mysterious truth, a life-altering truth. By the love and grace of God, we have what I'm going to call *the Christ-light*.

What Is the Christ-Light?

What exactly is this Christ-light? Well, it's a divine person, the person of Jesus Christ ruling in our hearts (Col. 3:15). But it also involves the work of all three persons in the Godhead. Let me explain.

In God's sovereignty, when you accepted Christ, he opened the door to your true, redeemed self. By the prompting and power of God's Spirit, you let him in. Jesus Christ now lives *in* you (Gal. 2:20; Rom. 8:10; 2 Cor. 4:6–7; Eph. 3:17; Col. 1:27). You are a home for another.

But at the same time, when Christ entered, he brought divine company. Jesus said he *and his Father* would make their home in you (John 14:23). In the same chapter, Jesus also promised to send another "Helper," the Spirit of truth, the Holy Spirit (14:16). The Spirit is our constant guide, working to shape us to the image of Christ by the will of our Father. Every Christian is a party of four.

What does all this have to do with light? We have to start by asking what it means for us to be indwelt by the persons of the Godhead. What difference does that make in us? That's worth a book in itself. But one way to understand it is to say that we now have the *will*, *heart*, and *work* of God inside us. These elements can be linked to the persons of the Godhead, though there is clear overlap, as there should be, for God is one. The *will* of God in the gospels is often associated with the God the Father (Matt. 7:21; Luke 10:21; John 5:19, 30; 6:38, 40), even though the Son and Spirit share this will. The *heart* of God is expressed in the Son, who gives us a whole new seat of emotion (Eph. 3:17), with godly desires and aspirations and longings. And the *work* of God is emphasized by the Spirit, who ceaselessly applies the good news of Christ to our hearts and minds (Ezek. 36:27; Gal. 5:22; 1 John 3:24). So, we can summarize salvation inside us with the words *will*, *heart*, and *work*.

Yet, it's with Christ and the heart that Scripture uses the imagery of light. In John's beautifully poetic prologue, he writes, "In him was life, and the life was the light of men. The light shines in the darkness, and the darkness has not overcome it" (John 1:4–5). Later in John's Gospel, Jesus calls himself the light of the world (John 8:12). In giving his light to us by abiding inside us, Christ *makes us* light—not by making us divine but by making us more like himself in love and holiness. Paul says that we are light in the Lord, and that the light of Christ shines on us (Eph. 5:8–14). In Romans 13:12, Paul talks about putting on "the armor of light," but this is bound up with putting on Christ himself. "To put on Christ is to be identified with him not only in his death but also in his resurrection. It is to be united to him in the likeness of his resurrection life."[2] This light of Christ's resurrection fills us with hope. That's why Paul also says that Christ in us, as the great mystery of the faith, is "the hope of glory" (Col. 1:27).

So, what is the Christ-light? *The Christ-light is our renewed Christ-governed heart, led by the will of the Father and worked in the power of the Spirit.* This Christ-light is so powerful that it makes us *new creatures* (2 Cor. 5:17). We are now marked by *love* (John 13:35) and filled with resurrection life and hope. Nothing could be greater, more mysterious, and more potent than this divine light. And as we'll see in a later chapter, the Christ-light draws our hearts to truth, love, and beauty.

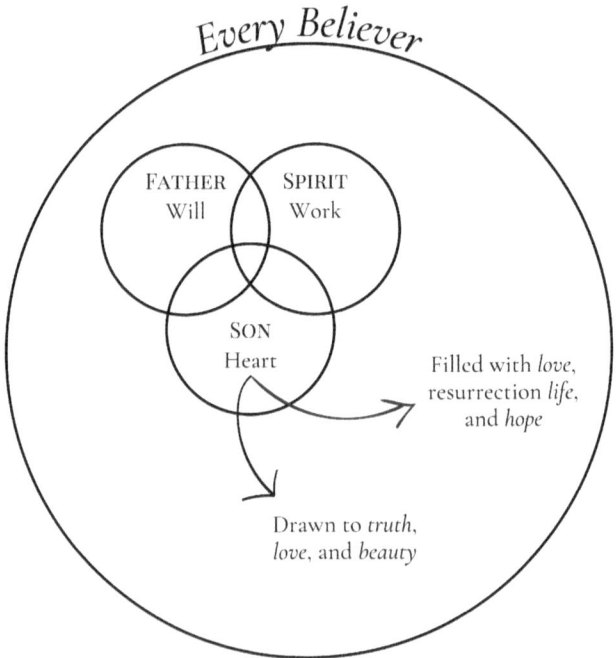

In the pages that follow we're going to see just how broad and deep the implications are for this Christ-light in Christian relationships—not in some abstract sense, but in the text message you send your mother, in the response to a friend who sees the world differently from you, even in the impulsive remark you want to make to someone who has completely misunderstood you, who thinks little of you, who wishes you harm. Yes, even here the Christ-light burns and beckons us to give ourselves, as Christ gave himself for us. Giving, as we'll see, is the hallmark of love.

But before exploring the implications of this Christ-light in daily life, we need to back up and start with understanding *God* as light. I believe we can't understand anything deeply apart from seeing its relation to him, even smaller subsets of theology and spirituality. God is the *who* that defines every *what*. We stare at him to understand anything. I say this because I come from a tradition of Reformed theology that places God at the center of everything. J. Gresham Machen, who founded the seminary where I serve, put it this way: "The relation to God is the all-important thing. It is not a mere means to an end. Everything else is secondary to it."[3] If we want to know anything truly, we start by knowing God. In the words of my Dutch elder brother, "God, and God only, has ultimate definitory power. God's description or plan of the fact makes the fact what it is."[4] If we want to know more deeply what this Christ-light is and what difference it makes in our lives, we have to start by staring at God and his plan to redeem all things through the Son and by the Spirit. So, we'll begin there in the next chapter.

Then in the following ones, we'll get into what happened at the fall (Gen. 3) and our lostness in the dark of sin, where we found ourselves before the Christ-light ignited us.

The remainder of the book will focus on how Jesus—the great candle for whom we all burn (Rom. 11:36)—interacted with God's people, the ones chosen in him before the foundation of the world. Jesus has the sole and divine ability to ignite souls in God's weary and wandering flock. Even in the worst and lowest of those chosen by God, Jesus drew near to give his Christ-light to them and to protect their flame from the wind of the world (John 16:33). He did things in, with, and for others that set them on holy fire, that brought them from death to life (John 5:24) and filled them with that resurrection hope we mentioned. And then he encouraged them to "walk in the light" he had given them (1 John 1:5–7), to hold high their new heart-aura and their hope of glory.

Why did God do this? Why? The reason is shrouded in his mysterious, sovereign, gracious will. We don't read, "For God so loved the world *because*..." We read, "For God so loved the world *that...*" (John 3:16). There's no reason given for *why* God loves, no quality in us that must be responsible for drawing him in.

This may seem tangential, but we can be tempted to identify something in *us* that draws God to us, whether that's our pitiable condition or our being made in God's image. But I've come to see that only God's mysterious, voluntary, choosing love is responsible for the Christ-light igniting our souls. The mystery here is meant to *stay*. Any attempt to shoulder it out of the picture with explanation is an exercise in futility and potentially hazardous theology.

After we look at the Christ-light and its relation to our being made in God's image, we'll spend the remaining words on how the light of the world engaged with others. This will serve as Spirit-driven inspiration for us as we interact with brothers and sisters in Christ each day. The point of studying vignettes of Jesus is to drive home the point: *we must learn to see the Christ-light in our faith-family*. We must learn to look at *them* and see *him*. Otherwise, we'll never learn to love as Christ loved. And that's no small thing, since Jesus himself said, "By this all people will know that you are my disciples, if you have love for one another" (John 13:35).

The Christ-Light Poem

Now, before we dive in, there was a poem at the outset of the book. I'm going to break the golden rule of poetry and give an explanation. I do this because the poem will serve you best if you know the theology behind it. Here it is again.

> God lit a candle in your chest.
> The wax is of the very best.
> The wick is woven strong, unbreaking,
> And the flame is of the Spirit's making.

Line 1. As we noted earlier, our triune God passed his light to you in Christ. He did it voluntarily, in the mystery of love, rooted in himself. He comes to us to bring rebirth (John 3) in the depth of his own overflowing self-love. As Vern Poythress writes, "God loves himself and is intimate with himself. We see this beauty and intimacy in the love of the Father for the Son (John 3:34–35), and the mutual love among all three persons of the Trinity. Out of the fullness of what God is, he displays himself in the world, and especially to human beings."[5] God's ancient and mysterious love is the only explanation for you and me receiving the Christ-light. This should lead us to humility, gratitude, and worship.

Line 2. Who you are now, your wax, is bound to Christ as the light of life (John 8:12), given by the will of the Father in the powerful working of his Spirit. You can no longer identify yourself apart from the Trinity who redeemed you in grace. As I've written elsewhere, *you* are *they*.[6] And yet because you are made of wax, God is going to keep shaping you in his light.

Line 3. The wick at your core—what holds the light—is the Spirit of Christ himself (Rom. 8:9), the light of the world (John 8:12), the one to whom we are all conforming in the grace of God (Rom. 8:29). We have *his* light in us, not our own. We are united to *his* flame.

Only those who believe in Jesus have his light inside them, guaranteeing by the Spirit their eternal communion with God. I say that the Son of God is the wick of our candle because it is only in him that we can do anything. He's the one who said, "apart from me you can do nothing" (John 15:5). We want to burn and shine in the darkness of our world because of *him*. Though we had all fallen (Rom. 3:23) and lived in the darkness (Eph. 5:8), the Son has secured our eternal illumination with the God of light since he has overcome the darkness we bowed down to (John 1:5; 16:33).

Line 4. Our flame as standing candles burns by the Spirit, the one who gave life and breath to the first human (Gen. 2:7), the one who breathes new life into us as we accept and embrace the warming light of Christ (Rom. 8:11). The Spirit represents our resurrection life, as the same Spirit who raised Christ from the dead. Even death has no power over this life inside us. We are eternally aflame.

You can read the poem now with a heightened sense of the goodness and mystery of God, the ancient Chandler, the one who will not quench even the faintest burning wick of his people (Isa. 42:3). It's with him that we begin, because with him all things begin.

REFLECT

1. Why do you think God put his Christ-light in you? (See Colossians 1:16 and Revelation 4:11.) Why does the Spirit work to brighten the light of Christ in us? (See John 3:16; 1 John 4:19.)[7]

2. If God has lit a candle in every follower of Christ, what does that suggest about our interactions with Christian brothers and sisters each day? What should we assume about them? How might our interactions with non-Christians differ?

3. What do you think it means to be made in God's image? Think not only about Genesis 1:26–27, but about all the ways in which we imitate God.

PRAY

God of light and love,
You are here, inside me,
Behind my pulsing heart.
Your presence is my life.
I *am* light in you,
And I can't be more myself
Unless I'm looking more like Christ.
Show me the light you put inside me.
And turn my chin up to see the light in my faith-family,
Rather than looking for their darkness.

THE GOD OF LIGHT

WHO IS GOD? No question could run deeper, span wider, or coast longer on the words of men. There's a rich deposit in Scripture of proper names and images. But given the theme of this book, let's consider God as *light*, or as James called him, "the Father of lights" (James 1:17).

> "The Father of lights"—that is your name,
> A blinding brilliance among heavenly hosts,
> For even angels with wings of flame
> Can't stare at Father, Son, and Holy Ghost.

Light is closely associated with that old word "glory." The Westminster Confession of Faith (2.2) says, "God hath all life, glory, goodness, blessedness, in and of himself; and is alone in and unto himself all-sufficient, not standing in need of any creatures which he hath made, nor deriving any glory from them, but only manifesting his own glory in, by, unto, and upon them."

That may sound stiff to today's ears—with all those "haths" and "untos." But think of it this way: God is the great, steadfast, immoveable light that shines behind and through this world. He is *radiant*. And that radiance touches everything, but it also radiates *from* those who hold Christ inside them.

The Nicene Creed calls Jesus Christ "God of God, Light of Light" because his brilliance as the eternal Son matches the joyfully blinding radiance of the Father and Spirit. This radiant God has filled the whole world with his light. In John Calvin's words, "Whichever way we turn our eyes, there is no part of the world, however small, in which at least some spark of God's glory does not shine. In particular, we cannot gaze at this beautiful masterpiece of the world, in all its length and breadth, without being completely dazed, as it were, by an endless flood of light."[8] *An endless flood of light*—that's the God who stands behind the world we wake to.

And yet you and I don't wake up blinded. Why? Well, God is a Spirit (John 4:24). We can't see spirits. So, while the God of radiance is blindingly bright, we walk through the world by *faith* in that light, believing that the Father of lights illumines all the things around us and even shines out from Christ inside us. This is deeply mysterious.

Herman Bavinck, perhaps my favorite theologian, wrote, "The spirituality of God refers to that perfection of God that describes him, negatively, as being immaterial and invisible, analogously to the spirit of angels and the souls of humans; and, positively, as the hidden, simple (uncompounded), absolute ground of all creatural, somatic, and pneumatic being."[9] Now that's a mouthful! Even my favorite theologians struggle to keep things "on the bottom shelf," as my mother says. Bavinck is just trying to argue that God as a Spirit is invisible and yet upholds everything we see. We might think of God as the light behind all earthly lights.[10]

And because of that behindness, because the Father of lights is hidden, we can be tempted to think he isn't really here. That, I argue in another book, is Satan's great lie, the lie that tells us to live *as if* God weren't really present.[11] The great truth is that God is always present; he's always the Light behind all lesser lights. Our awareness of him is a matter of Spirit-gifted faith, a certainty in what we cannot see (Heb. 11:1).

What It Means

But what, more specifically, does it mean to say that God is light? We need to think about this so we have a sense of all the meaning that bursts from the concept of being made in his image and receiving the Christ-light (the topic of the next chapter).[12] God as light can mean many things. But for the sake of focus, let's rest for now on three qualities clearly linked with physical light: *truth, warmth* (love), and *beauty*.

Truth. The radiance of God lets us see what *is*, what's real. Just as a light in a darkened room shows us what's there, God shows us the furniture of life, all the things we lean on for stability and meaning: who we are, where we stand, where we're headed, what matters most, what we should strive for. Bavinck puts it this way, "Light in Scripture is the image of truth, holiness, and blessedness (Ps. 43:3; Isa. 10:17; Ps. 97:11)."[13] God shines to show us what is true, sacred, and good. Elsewhere Bavinck writes, "What light is in the natural world—the source of knowledge, purity, and joy—God is in the world of the spirit."[14] God is the light of truth, the one who shows us *all*, because the Son who lives in our hearts *is* all in all (1 Cor. 15:28). He helps us see what's around us, as well as our true spiritual condition. I've always loved how Charles Wesley expressed this in the great hymn "And Can It Be,"

> Long my imprisoned spirit lay
> Fast bound in sin and nature's night;
> Thine eye diffused a quick'ning ray,
> I woke, the dungeon flamed with light;
> My chains fell off, my heart was free;
> I rose, went forth and followed Thee.

"The dungeon flamed with light" points both to where our spirits are in the grips of sin, and also to the saving presence of God that calls us deeper into his marvelous illumination (1 Pet. 2:9), the Christ-light. In sum, God as the true light shows us *who* and *where* we really are.

Warmth. As light brings heat, warming the blood within birds and the chlorophyll in praying blades of grass, God as the Father of light warms us in his love. And we desperately want that, don't we? Rich Villodas writes, "The fractures within and around us don't feel right because our souls desire bonds of belonging and belovedness."[15] We want belonging and belovedness. We want *God's* love more than anything. In fact, the love of God is the beating heart of creation. Love is God's identity, our highest calling, and the power beneath every mountain range and rolling sea. Robert Letham links this especially to God's trinitarian nature—three persons in eternal, loving relationship. "The Trinity means love is at the heart of the cosmos that God made. It is not a cold, heartless universe of pointlessness and futility, but it has a purpose that God has designed for it from eternity. Since God is personal, he is love, the living God, for life and love go together."[16]

Life and love go together because that's who *God* is. His warmth of love does more than give us a purpose; it *changes* us. Writing of Romans 8:29, John Murray says, "God's love is not passive emotion; it is active volition and it moves determinatively to nothing less than the highest goal conceivable for his adopted children, conformity to the image of the only-begotten Son."[17] Take a moment to marvel at that—*the highest conceivable goal*. The warmth of God's love changes us, as a flame melting wax, shaping us to God himself in the person of the Son. If the truth of God helps us see who and where we are, the warmth or love of God swells our hearts with praise and adoration. Once we were blind, but now we see (John 9:25). And so we do as George Herbert directs,

> All knees shall bow to thee; all wits shall rise,
> And praise him who did make and mend our eyes.[18]

Beauty. God as light gives us truth, and he gives us the warmth of his self-conforming love. But he is also the most beautiful and the source of all the beauty we see around us. That God is the most beautiful might not strike us as clearly biblical in terms of the language, but "for the beauty of God Scripture has a special word: glory."[19] And Scripture harps on God's glory so much that we must say God is "the pinnacle of beauty, the beauty toward which all creatures point."[20] Every instance of beauty around us is an index finger pointing to God. Ignoring creaturely manifestations of beauty thus amounts to ignoring the beauty of God. One author wrote, "If the beauty within creation points us to the beautiful one, then when we fail to behold and respond to that beauty, we hide ourselves from him."[21] And the beauty of God burns most luminously when we understand that life is not about *us* seeking him out but about *him* seeking us out. This is what God does in Christ—in that deep and mysterious love we've talked about. The Christ-light opens our eyes to the giver of beauty. "Christ is the answer to the desires which emerge from our deepest parts. We long for beauty because we long for the one who is the source of beauty and who calls us back to life through the means of beauty in our lives."[22]

Let me offer an example of how God's beauty can overwhelm us and call us deeper into himself.[23]

In the fading daylight of a late October afternoon, I drove to Hamilton's, an apple orchard a few miles from our home. Winding my car around the bends and curves of farming fields, I was rushing. Hamilton's closed at 4:00pm. It was 3:40pm. After that day, they would be closed for the season.

I sped down their little driveway and rolled across the parking field, soaked in golden sunlight. I sprinted to the stand, looking for pre-picked apples. They had none. I'd have to pick my own in five minutes flat. So, I wheeled my basket right to the rows for golden delicious—23 and 24—and started picking like a madman, hugging the apples off the trees in bunches.

How many miracles had my tires tread over and my feet stomped on so far? Probably billions—caterpillars trekking over the pavement on a perilous journey to the world across a giant "noise path"; bees woken by an unexpected warmth from the great golden orb; resilient blades of grass seeming to lose everything as I crushed them, only to rise again like Job from the whirlwind. Most miracles of beauty are trampled. We go too fast to notice them.

But there was this moment when God seemed to pause time. Pushing through several branches to get at an apple toward the top of a tree, I plucked it from the stem as the sun poured in all around my hands. The pulling released a tiny cloud of pollen, drifting into the light in a dazed dance. The particles were so effortless, these tiny sails for sunlight, swirling around my right hand like a song. And I stopped. I stopped because I was overwhelmed with beauty, enraptured by the gardening God who drew my too-frenzied eyes to *this* little orchestra of dust, this infinitesimal suite of dancers, content to float and twirl and then settle back onto the leaves and branches . . . a song of golden smoke.

The whole experience made me wonder how *anyone* on the planet could cease to marvel, could even *pretend* to have a grip on the intricate magnificence what's going on all around them. It makes me think of Mary Oliver's poem, "Mysteries, Yes."

> Let me keep my distance, always, from those
> who think they have the answers.
> Let me keep company always with those who say
> "Look!" and laugh in astonishment,
> and bow their heads.[24]

And so I respond in verse.

> A God of grace and golden apples,
> A king of light and trees and flowers,
> Who makes the pollen dust his chapels
> To fill with songs of daylight hours.
> Your beauty is too great to gather.
> As we rush through the pulsing wild,
> Ignoring all. Why would you rather
> Give us more than make us mild?
> Pause the world. Let turning stop.
> Halt rash feet and fumbling fingers.
> Instead of deluge, give one drop,
> And slow our hearts to let it linger.

What sort of God is this, who makes a billion miracles, knowing we may only trip over *one*? Who sheds the trees of their colored autumn hands after hearing a thousand ovations from the summer canopy? Who builds chapels from apple dust and brings an orchestra to float on a tree branch? Who gives *all* and seems to ask so little in return?

God as light is the giver of truth, love, and beauty. This is the one in whose image we are made. At our best, we are, as Joel Clarkson put it, "*illuminated images*, made to reflect the divine light of Jesus to a world in need, acting as sacred depictions of God's love which might redirect longing eyes toward the fulfillment of their desires in him."[25]

But what does it mean to bear God's image? What light did we lose at the fall that called for the Christ-light to save us from cold chaos? That's where we go next.

REFLECT

1. What other qualities of God come to mind when you think of him as "light"?

2. How does the nature of God as light (truth, warmth, beauty) influence and change us?

3. Why do you think we overlook the beauty of God around us?

PRAY

> Father of lights,
> Son of wonder,
> Spirit of life,
> You show me what's true.
> You show me your love.
> You show me your beauty.
> Make me enraptured by you.
> Burn so brightly
> That all lesser lights
> Seem like shadows in comparison.

Help me to trust in you
As the Light *behind* all lights.

CREATURES OF LIGHT, FALLEN AND REDEEMED

BEFORE SIN ENTERED THE world, we had a kind of light inside us. We can't say much about this light, since Scripture doesn't. But we have to infer this from a passage such as Romans 1:21. How could our hearts become "darkened" if they weren't somehow lit in the first place? Heart and mind darkness is a form of judgment for sin (Rom. 11:9–11; Eph. 4:18). So, before sin was in the world, we carried some kind of light in us, a sort of candle. The giving of that light, of course, was still an act of grace on God's part. We did nothing to "earn" this light. All components of our life and being are divine gifts. We are lesser lights from the greater Light, blessed with a glow only because God willed this in his mysterious love. As Herman Bavinck put it, God "is the Sun of being and all creatures are His fleeting rays."[26] Rays of light owe all to the source. While this light we carried before the fall was only a pure gift of grace, it was nevertheless true and beautiful as a reflection of God. As the jewel of creation, we were "good" little lights (Gen. 1:31).

Being "Good" as Walking in Light

But what does it mean to be "good"? Given how much we use that word, it's difficult to pin down a meaning. And while I would argue that this is part of the beauty of language (being inherently mysterious as a reflection of God himself), many people settle on only one perspective, one facet of the meaning.[27] Being good means being *obedient*, or *kind*, or *selfless*. These are all true, of course. But let's broaden our approach using the metaphor we've developed so far. Let's link *good* with the word *light*. We can also tie it to *communion*, since our possession of light only holds in our relationship to the God of light.

When we looked at God as light, we focused on the concepts of *truth*, *love*, and *beauty*. Just as we base our understanding of these words on God himself, who has given us the gift of language, we can examine the word "good" in the context of who God is.[28] The meaning of any word "is related to the fact that God knows everything."[29] God's knowledge, in other words, defines the meanings of our words. This certainly brings in mystery, since we can't know everything God knows, nor can we know things *in the way* God knows them. And yet, through God's Son, the expression of the Father's thought in the power of the Spirit, we can know things truly.[30] As odd as it may sound, we look to the Trinity to understand the meaning of any word, including the word "good."

Goodness is a reflection of the *harmony* in the Godhead. It emphasizes God's own approval of himself. That can sound very strange to readers. Is God divinely egotistical? No. He is the purest, highest form of self-giving love. The Father loves and gives himself to the Son. The Son loves and gives himself to the Father. The Spirit loves and gives himself to the Father and the Son. In this eternal love and self-giving, there is perfect harmony—a harmony that transcends all of our earthly portrayals. God himself looks on that harmony with a holy headnod. He gives approval to the beautiful and perfect harmony in himself. That harmony is *good*. Is there mystery here? Certainly. Do we fully understand what we are saying? No. That's part of what it means to be a limited creature trying to worship an unlimited God. There are times when describing things is better than trying to define them with perfect precision (we can't do the latter anyway). This is one of those times.

So, when God called his creation *good*, when he said that the completed work of his mouth was "very good" (Gen. 1:31), what was he saying about us? He was saying that we were made in *harmony* with himself, in perfect fellowship with him. We weren't independent. We were beautifully *dependent* on him. This is before the entrance of sin. "Even while human beings were innocent, God intended that they should not live independently of him. He created us to have communion with him."[31]

Being "good," living in harmony with God, meant that we walked in his light, stepping into the truth, love, and beauty he shared with us. That's why the New Testament speaks of our restoration as the act of "walking in the light" (Ps. 56:13; 89:15; Isa. 2:5; 9:2; John 8:12; 12:35–36). John says, "But if we walk in the light, as he is in the light, we have fellowship with one another, and the blood of Jesus his Son cleanses us from all sin" (1 John 1:7). Can you see how light comes together with fellowship, with communion? Our walking in the light leads to communion with each other, and that communion is a reflection of the God of light, who perfectly communes with himself. That's what it meant for us to be good. We shared in God's light because we were in perfect harmony with him. This is perhaps one of the greatest truths lost in the Western world bent on individualism and independence. Harmony with God *gives* light, because God *is* light.

> What mystery lies beyond the hills
> Before we came, before we stepped,
> Before we dressed in selfish wills
> And clung to what cannot be kept?
> That three are one, and gave and loved;
> That holding harmony let off light;
> That truth and beauty were not gloved,
> But let us touch and hold them tight.

Our Darkening and Corruption

But our God-given glow in harmony was short-lived. The entrance of sin brought darkness; it extinguished the candle inside us. But it didn't just take away the light; it left a noxious trail of smoke, always poisoning and corrupting what's around us.

Sin brought darkness, but it also brought full depravity. In other words, our sin wasn't just the absence of light; it was the corruption and rebellion that bled into the air from our doused wick. This squares with Paul's description of our depraved, darkened state in Romans 3:10–18.

> As it is written: "None is righteous, no, not one; no one understands; no one seeks for God. All have turned aside; together they have become worthless; no one does good, not even one. Their throat is an open grave; they use their tongues to deceive. The venom of asps is under their lips. Their mouth is full of curses and bitterness. Their feet are swift to shed blood; in their paths are ruin and misery, and the way of peace they have not known. There is no fear of God before their eyes."

Not a flattering description of lit wicks once resembling God, is it? But that's what happened when sin entered the world. As Paul put it in Ephesians 5:8, we *became* darkness. And our doused wicks wafted in the black.

WHERE THE IMAGE OF GOD FITS

It's in this context that discussions of "the image of God" (*imago Dei*) become so important. The opening chapter concerning the Christ-light makes sense based on (1) who we were created to be (little lights in harmony with God) and (2) on what happened when sin entered the picture (we became darkness). The Christ-light is a portrayal, a biblical summary, of our redemption. But we can't understand redemption without knowing where we began. And now we find ourselves living in a world that desperately needs the light of God that we hold within us by grace. How are we to act now?

We can get at this from another angle. Theologians discuss the image of God largely because they're concerned with who we were made to be, who we are apart from redemption, and who we are after we accept Christ and the Spirit works in us. *Identity* is central to all of this. And identity is a complex but pivotal issue for every generation. How we understand the image of God thus informs our sense of history, our present purpose, and our future destiny. In short, it's all-encompassing. How can we navigate a topic like this? We can't cover everything. And I don't aim to. Instead, I'd like to describe the image of God more broadly as the *imitation of God* and more narrowly through the terms *covenant*, *communion*, and *revelation*. There's a lot to discuss, and we'll have to be selective. That's why I think of the image of God as a candle wick with many threads. Let's start there, and then move from the broader to the narrower.

The Image of God as a Many-Threaded Wick

Of the many ways in which we could understand the image of God in us, I'd like to focus on that analogy—a candle wick woven from many threads. The meaning of the image of God is a topic that could fill libraries—not just because there are so many competing claims about the "one thing" the image of God means, but because Scripture as a whole calls us beyond simple definitions.[32] Bearing God's image means that we holistically resemble him, that we *imitate* him in every creaturely way possible. There are lots of ways to explore this, but I've recently read of using what T. P. Yates calls *lex Christi*, the law of Christ.[33] This approach takes the Ten Commandments and uses them as perspectives on our relationship to God and our behavior in the world. Vern Poythress even links *lex Christi* to the image of God, illustrating how the Commandments each offer a perspective on how we imitate God, that is, how we bear God's image. Below is a summary, including each commandment, the attribute of God it highlights, how we imitate God in that area, and how we rebel against God in sin.[34]

Commandment (Exod. 20)	Attribute of God	How We Imitate	How We Rebel
"You shall have no other gods before me" (v. 3).	God's supremacy	Affirming God's supremacy and exercising our loving stewardship over creation (creaturely supremacy)	Treating other things (gods) as more supreme than God
"You shall not make for yourself a carved image, or any likeness of anything that is in heaven above, or that is in the earth beneath, or that is in the water under the earth" (v. 4).	God's holiness	Affirming God's holiness and keeping ourselves holy	Giving god-like status to anything else in our life; defiling ourselves through sin
"You shall not take the name of the Lord your God in vain" (v. 7).	God's blessedness (and the source of all blessing)	Honoring God's name; blessing others in his name	Misusing God's name or cursing him; cursing rather than blessing others
"Remember the Sabbath day, to keep it holy. 9 Six days you shall labor, and do all your work, 10 but the seventh day is a Sabbath to the Lord your God" (vv. 8–10).	God's dynamism and power	Affirming God's power and constant work; trusting in his control over all things and resting in that trust	Ignoring or downplaying God's power; trusting only ourselves (never resting)
"Honor your father and your mother, that your days may be long in the land that the Lord your God is giving you" (v. 12).	God's relational harmony	Honoring God's loving relationship with us; striving to keep harmonious relationships with others	Rejecting God's relationship with us; creating discord in earthly relationships

Commandment (Exod. 20)	Attribute of God	How We Imitate	How We Rebel
"You shall not murder" (v. 13).	God's life-giving and sustaining nature	Honoring God as life-giver; protecting human life and other created life forms	Taking life
"You shall not commit adultery" (v. 14).	God's loving intimacy and omnipresence (always being with his beloved)	Affirming God's loving intimacy in marriage	Committing adultery, encouraging discord in marriages, or belittling divorce
"You shall not steal" (v. 15).	God's generosity	Affirming God's giving and responding with gratitude and worship	Being withholding, selfish, or covetous
"You shall not bear false witness against your neighbor" (v. 16).	God's truthfulness	Affirming the truth of God's words and upholding the truth among others	Doubting the truthfulness of God, spreading falsehoods about God and others
"You shall not covet your neighbor's house; you shall not covet your neighbor's wife, or his male servant, or his female servant, or his ox, or his donkey, or anything that is your neighbor's" (v. 17).	God's contentedness	Affirming that God is sufficient for your life and for all those around you	Envying others or seeking to satisfy yourself with things rather than with God

Imitating God through the Lex Christi

I'm not diving into the specifics here, because my goal is to show two simple things through this broader discussion of the image of God as *imitation*.

First, when we image God in any of these ways (and in ways not stated here), the other means of imaging God don't disappear. They hover in the background. For example, when I love my wife by speaking well of her to others, that's related to God's loving intimacy and the human institution of marriage that reflects him. But I'm also affirming God's supremacy by honoring his word, affirming his holiness by guarding the covenant of marriage he instilled (Gen. 2:24), honoring God's name by blessing my wife in a way that relates to God's blessing of me, and so on. *We're always either imitating or rebelling against God somehow in all that we do*, usually in more ways than we can realize.

Second, it's evident from the full teaching of Scripture that we image God in *many* ways. All of these ways—even those we haven't explored—represent the many-threaded "wick" we have in bearing God's image.

I'd like to choose a few strands of this threaded wick to help us better understand the fall and our need for the Christ-light: our *covenant* with God established by his revelation, our desire to be close to him (*communion*), and our constant *reactions* to God in the world and in his word. Looking at these three threads is how I'm narrowing our focus a bit.

Joining the Mediterranean with France and the Netherlands

Again, tomes have been written on what it means to bear God's image.[35] We would gain much from exploring that continent of prayerful research and writing. But now that we've established that bearing God's image means that we holistically imitate him, I'll just be presenting a few threads in the wick from my own theological tradition, drawing on the Apostle Paul, John Calvin, Geehardus Vos, and Cornelius Van Til—a Mediterranean, a Frenchman, and two Dutchmen. Looking at these strands of the image of God will help us understand how the fall *darkened* us and how we need the Christ-light.

Before unpacking this, I should say that theologians often speak of the image of God in a broader and narrower sense.[36] As noted earlier, they do this mainly to clarify what happened when sin entered the picture—who we were before the fall, who we were after it, and who we are now in Christ. What elements of our being made in God's image remained after the fall? What was lost? What does redemption in Christ look like? These aren't simple questions. They have countries beneath them, but now is not the place to traverse all the territory. Suffice it to say that I believe the image of God in us was *marred* by the fall but not *erased*. In fact, our ability to image God is the very thing that Paul says leaves us "without excuse" for not acknowledging and worshiping him.

Now, brace yourself a bit for some quotations as we try to see the themes of *covenant, communion,* and *revelation* in a selection of figures.

The Apostle Paul

In Romans 1, Paul argues that we are *covenantal* creatures. In other words, we're creatures who have been born into a relationship with God. We all enter existence this way because of God's revelation. This is Paul's point in Romans 1:18–21.

> For the wrath of God is revealed from heaven against all ungodliness and unrighteousness of men, who by their unrighteousness suppress the truth. For what can be known about God is plain to them, because God has shown it to them. For his invisible attributes, namely, his eternal power and divine nature, have been clearly perceived, ever

> since the creation of the world, in the things that have been made. So they are without excuse. For although they knew God, they did not honor him as God or give thanks to him, but they became futile in their thinking, and their foolish hearts were darkened.

"The things that have been made" means everything. Everything around us reveals God (Ps. 19:1–4). That means we're born into a God-reflecting atmosphere, and so by default we're born into a relationship with him, a covenant. And that covenant has relational requirements for us. That's why Paul says people are "without excuse." Without excuse for what? John Murray says we're without an excuse for *not* offering God glory, thought, affection, devotion, and gratitude.[37] That's a full description of *relationship*, isn't it? In short form, we might say we're responsible for acknowledging God's presence (as the glorious, great, awe-inspiring Creator) and being faithful to him (in thought, affection, and devotion). That's what it means to be in a covenant: to recognize the presence of another and act in faithfulness according to the relational boundaries. That's the message of this Mediterranean man of God. Now, on to the Frenchman.

John Calvin

What did it mean for Calvin that we are made in God's image? Following Romans 1, Calvin affirms that we have *clear knowledge of God*. Everyone, without exception, knows God. He sometimes called this the *sense of divinity* or a *feeling for divinity*.

> We regard it as beyond dispute that there is in the mind of man, by natural inclination, a certain feeling for divinity, so that no one should seek refuge by claiming ignorance. The Lord has instilled in everyone some understanding of his majesty, so

> that all, having learned that there is one God and that he is their creator, should be condemned by their own testimony because they have failed to honor him and to devote their lives to doing his will.[38]

Calvin is holding on to Paul's coattails. But notice that this "feeling for divinity" or seed of divinity (*sensus divinitatis*) is something implanted *in* us, drawn out by God's all-encompassing self-revelation. Paul says that God reveals himself "in the things that have been made" (Rom. 1:20). Again, that's everything—every change in Pennsylvania topography, every maple tree, every fragile bee's wing and silk peony petal. Every person, too. Yes, God even reveals himself *in* our conscience and in the beauty of our thoughts—provided that those thoughts are bent towards him. God's revelation soaks through the varied garments of creation and all those who stand within it.

This re-sounds the truth already present in Romans 1: From our very inception, we are creatures in *covenant* with God, creatures bound to him in relationship. "We were created as covenant beings," K. Scott Oliphint writes.[39] I'll say it again: you and I are *covenant creatures*, relational beings bound to the God of light—the source of truth, love, and beauty. And because we're bound to him, we'll never rid ourselves of our longing for him. That brings us to the first Dutchman.

Geerhardus Vos

Geerhardus Vos would certainly agree with the Apostle Paul, and John Calvin's understanding of him. But he adds a personal dimension to this—a screaming need in our time. If we bear God's image, if we all know him deep down because we're surrounded by his revelation without and within, then we must have a longing for him, an irrevocable desire for closeness with God. Theologians talk of this as our desire for *communion*. Look at what Vos says.

> That man bears God's image means much more than that he is spirit and possesses understanding, will, etc. It means above all that he is disposed for communion with God, that all the capacities of his soul can act in a way that corresponds to their destiny only if they rest in God. . . . According to the deeper Protestant conception, the image does not exist only in correspondence with God but in being disposed toward God. God's nature is, as it were, the stamp; our nature is the impression made by this stamp. Both fit together.[40]

Disposed for communion with God—ever leaning toward him in all things, always longing to fit perfectly together.

You've felt it, haven't you? A sense of lostness, of walking through the world as a pilgrim, of longing to dwell fully and ceaselessly with your maker? Each of us is a palace that wants to be inhabited, and we know who the inhabitants should be—Father, Son, and Holy Ghost, the center of all relationships, the Lord of lights, who cannot be opposed, not even by the dark of death. Unceasing communion with the God of truth, love, and beauty is what makes our heart chambers pulse. It's what gave us our light to begin with. George Herbert wrote,

> Since then, my God, thou hast
> So brave a palace built; O dwell in it,
> That it may dwell with thee at last!
> Till then, afford us so much wit;
> That, as the world serves us, we may serve thee,
> And both thy servants be.[41]

We're covenant creatures, but we're also communion-seekers. That's why we're here, and it's where we're going. As Kelly Kapic wrote, "Communion with God points not simply toward human origins but toward human ends, to the culmination and purpose of human creation."[42]

Now, on to the last Dutchman.

Cornelius Van Til

The second Dutchman follows the first, but what he added was an emphasis on our *reaction* to God's revelation. Born into covenant and driven toward communion with God, each of us is always *reacting* to the truth, love, and beauty of God surrounding us—God's revelation. "Man is always reacting ethically to this revelation of God. He first lives under the *general favor* of God and reacts favorably. Then he reacts unfavorably and comes under the curse of God."[43] We're always reacting or responding ethically to God—either in faithfulness or frustrated rebellion. There is no middle ground. Even inside us we have God's constant revelation to react to: in our conscience, in our longing for truth, love, and beauty. Van Til continues, "The Holy Spirit testifies to man through his own constitution as well as through the facts of the universe around him, that he is God's offspring and should act as such."[44]

We often feel as if we're in some sort of neutral middle space with God—neither for him nor against him. But Van Til was adamant about the falsehood of that feeling. We are always reacting to God because he's always addressing us, showing himself to us, putting himself in our path.

This is especially true in our thinking. We assume there are "good" thoughts and then there are "bad" thoughts, and then there are "neutral" thoughts floating somewhere in the middle. But Van Til's friend John Murray wrote in his commentary on Romans, "The mind of man is never a religious vacuum; if there is the absence of the true, there is always the presence of the false."[45] We are always reacting positively or negatively to the God of light. Always.

So, those are three strands in the many-threaded wick of God's image—part of what it means for us to be photons of a luminous Lord. *We are covenantal, communion-bent reactors to the pervasive revelation of God.* That's my synthesis of a Mediterranean, a Frenchman, and a pair of Dutchmen.

Each of these strands of God's image is wrapped up with the *lex Christi* components we looked at earlier. For example, covenant is related to God's supremacy (since he initiated the covenant) and God's relational harmony. It's also related to God's holiness, since keeping the covenant expresses our holiness. Likewise, our longing for communion is related to God's blessedness, since communion with God is the greatest blessing. It's also clearly related to God's relational harmony. And because we have *life* in communion with God, it's related to God's life-giving and life-sustaining nature. All of these strands are woven together, perspectives on perspectives on perspectives. Before the fall, our imaging of God was a glorious wick—an unbroken, many-faceted fellowship with the God of life and light. Adam and Eve walked around the garden with God, imitating him as children do with their parents. *His* light was *their* light.

Losing the Light: Breaking Covenant and Communion

But then Genesis 3 happened. All those ways in which we can *rebel* against God rather than *imitate* him became a reality. Our wick went out, and noxious fumes rose from us constantly. We became both darkened and corrupting. We didn't *lose* the wick, mind you. We still bore God's image in a general sense, but the wick was doused, and poison came where godly passion had been. Where light had lived, now darkness reigned. By breaking covenant and communion with God—in an effort to become *like* God—we entered what Paul would eventually call "the domain of darkness" (Col. 1:13), a shadow kingdom.

In this shadow kingdom, we weren't just partially blinded or misled. We became corpses, physically alive but spiritually dead. That's stark language, but it's the language God uses through the Apostle Paul. We were *dead*. Any good we did was either a gift of God's common grace (i.e., anything good we receive apart from salvation in Christ), or a grace-infused bestowal of blessing by the promises of God, which would one day be fulfilled in his

Son. This is how Paul summarizes things in the second chapter of Ephesians.

> And you were dead in the trespasses and sins in which you once walked, following the course of this world, following the prince of the power of the air, the spirit that is now at work in the sons of disobedience—among whom we all once lived in the passions of our flesh, carrying out the desires of the body and the mind, and were by nature children of wrath, like the rest of mankind. But God, being rich in mercy, because of the great love with which he loved us, even when we were dead in our trespasses, made us alive together with Christ—by grace you have been saved—and raised us up with him and seated us with him in the heavenly places in Christ Jesus, so that in the coming ages he might show the immeasurable riches of his grace in kindness toward us in Christ Jesus. (Eph. 2:1–7)

Note several things here. First, in our spiritual death, as smoking wicks poisoning a God-atmosphere (Acts 17:28), we were following "the prince of the power of the air," that is, Satan. Once again, there are only two spiritual directions open to us as creatures of God: towards him or away from him, under his rule or under the rule of his adversary. There is no neutrality. We are either illuminating or darkening.

Second, the motive behind our salvation is again only explained by God's mysterious *love* (v. 4), something that cannot be earned in any way, but can only be given in his sovereign will.

Third, we were made "alive together with Christ." But who is Christ? No library could do that question justice, but we at least know that he is the *light* (John 1:5; 8:12). If we're made alive together with Christ, then we have *his* light inside us. Our wick has been lit by God—first in creation and then again in re-creation! No more domain of darkness. No more noxious fumes. Something deeper and brighter burns in us now, something strange and powerful. More specifically, having the light of Christ inside us means we share his *heart* and *will*. Our life becomes driven by Christ's life, in his heart for sinners and his will to follow the Father in the faithfulness of the Spirit. As Rankin Wilbourne wrote, "God has called you into a new life, rooted in a history that predates you, anchored in the life, death, and resurrection of Jesus. . . . The lifeblood of another flows within you and gives you life. . . . You no longer belong only to yourself. Your identity now includes another; it is broadened from 'me' to 'us.'"[46]

Paul describes this in Colossians as a "rich and glorious mystery." Look at what he says.

> Now I rejoice in my sufferings for your sake, and in my flesh I am filling up what is lacking in Christ's afflictions for the sake of his body, that is, the church, of which I became a minister according to the stewardship from God that was given to me for you, to make the word of God fully known, the mystery hidden for ages and generations but now revealed to his saints. To them God chose to make known how great among the Gentiles are the riches of the glory of this mystery, which is Christ in you, the hope of glory. (Col. 1:24–27)

That's the Christ-light! It's a person, who *is* light, giving light and life to us. And a major component of that light is the hope of resurrection. Elsewhere Paul talks about "putting on Christ." And "to put on Christ is to be identified with him not only in his death but also in his resurrection. It is to be united to him in the likeness of his resurrection life."[47] *The likeness of his resurrection life*—think about what that means. Christ's resurrection life walked back through the door of death and shattered its shadowy threshold. Christ's resurrection life answered the ancient hope of every human being. "Yes, you will be forever with God.

You will be more than okay. You will be radiant and never alone. You will live *in* the light, *as* the light. No more darkness." Praise God for the riches and glory of this mystery!

It's only in Christ that our wick can be lit. Apart from him, we trudge through the shadow kingdom. What does that trudging mean, specifically? If we look at the strands we examined earlier, it means at least three things (much more could be gleaned from applying the *lex Christi*).

Covenant (knowledge and heart-darkness). Though we all *know* God deep down (Rom. 1:21), the fall led to our minds being broken and our hearts being darkened. We suppress the truth about God (1:18), and that leads to both our minds and our hearts falling into the shadow kingdom. Concerning fallen creatures of God, Murray notes, "reason estranged from the source of light led them into a delirium of vanity."[48] We began to use our minds to seek out and protect things other than God. And that is, as Murray so wonderfully phrases it, *a delirium of vanity*. Our heart, as "the seat of feeling, intellect, and will" fell into darkness.[49] We felt dark things. We thought dark things. We willed dark things. Dark. Dark. Dark. Could rebellion against the God of light be anything else?

Communion. We were made as communion-seeking creatures, but our rebellion clashed with God's relational harmony. We became restless, searching for relational fulfillment everywhere *except* in the one who could give us peace: God himself.

Reaction. Our default mode for reacting to God's relation became completely negative. Paul says that apart from God's saving work in Christ, we are *unable* to please God. He refers to those in the shadow kingdom as being "in the flesh." "For the mind that is set on the flesh is hostile to God, for it does not submit to God's law; indeed, it cannot. Those who are in the flesh cannot please God" (Rom. 8:7–8).

Yet, in Christ, we are not only reversed, walking back to the garden of Eden; we are *advanced*, moved to a place brighter than even Adam could fathom. That's because we not only walk in the kingdom of light, but the kingdom of light walks *inside* us. As covenant creatures, we are in full good standing with God, for Christ has fulfilled the covenant on our behalf and atoned for all of our sin. Our minds are being restored so that we will come to have "the mind of Christ" (1 Cor. 2:16). And our hearts are *new*. God has performed spiritual surgery on us. He took out the dark, dead heart. And he put a pulsing one inside (Ezek. 11:19; 36:26; Jer. 31:33; Heb. 8:10). On that new heart, a heart pumping with the life-giving blood of Christ, God *wrote* his law, the law of Christ, the *lex Christi*. *We are written.*

Christ has also opened the way to communion with God, making it possible for us to be one with him (John 17). That incessant yearning for belovedness and belonging, to be fully known and fully loved, and to pursue the greatest love of all without hindrance, is fulfilled in Christ, guaranteed by the Spirit in us right now (2 Cor. 1:22). We are on a road to oneness with God, even experiencing a foretaste of that oneness now, and there's no stopping us. We are with God because God is in us. There can be no separation. We then grow in the practice of speaking to God and hearing him speak back to us in his word, drawing nearer to him, so close that we can say with Paul, "It is no longer I who live, but Christ who lives in me" (Gal. 2:20). In short, Christ daily enacts a divine equation in our souls: communication + communion = union.[50]

Reaction. Because the Christ-light is in us, we can walk *as* children of light. We are light "in the Lord" (Eph. 5:8). We shine amidst the darkness of a crooked generation (Phil. 2:15). We are children of "the day," not of darkness or the night (1 Thess. 5:5). Our reaction to God's revelation all around us and inside us can now be faithful, full of hope, a hope for glory (Col. 1:27). That doesn't mean we're perfect. But it does mean we have the perfect persons of the Godhead indwelling us. Little by little, we're learning what it's like to walk through the world each day and react *in faithfulness* to what God has put around us and inside us, relying on the light of Christ.

CARRYING THE CHRIST-LIGHT: A WORD JOURNEY

It's still a bit cryptic, though, this Christ-light. What does it look like to carry *a person* inside us,[51] to have our wick relit by God, to be a house for the hope of glory? I can suggest what it means, but that won't eclipse any of the mystery. The greatest stories ever told always retain that element of mystery. Should the story of our lives be any different?

It's helpful to portray the carrying of the Christ-light inside us as a *word journey*. It was *through* words that we learned of Christ. It's *by* words that the Spirit grows and shapes us. And it's *in* words that we place our hope as we gaze at the promises of God. God's words impart the Christ-light to us and carry us through until our final day on earth. As the psalmist wrote, "The unfolding of your words gives light" (Ps. 119:130).

This begins with us recognizing that in Christ we have a new *identity*, given to us by the Spirit in the words of salvation. This new identity changes how we act in the world (think of the *reaction* element in our image of God discussion). Dallas Willard writes,

> God speaks not just for us and our purposes, nor does he speak primarily for our prosperity, safety or gratification. Those who receive the grace of God's saving companionship in his word are by that fact also fitted to show humankind how to live. They, and they alone, are at home in the universe as it actually is. In that sense they are the light of the world. Their transformed nature automatically suits them to this task. Therefore, this task is not an option or afterthought. The light that they radiate is not what they do but who they *are*.[52]

We *are* light in Christ (Eph. 5:8). It's not just a moral transformation, a behavior change. It's an identity metamorphosis. We are new creatures in the light of Christ (2 Cor. 5:17). And this new identity is meant to draw others to him. There is a missional focus here. Our new life and light *shows* and *shines*. "Only by *showing* how to live can we teach how to live. It is by the *kind of life* that is in us and that makes us examples of God's indwelling that we reveal the foundation for communicating God's redeeming word and Spirit to an ever-larger circle of human beings."[53]

So, we have a new identity as light-bearers, an identity imparted by words. That still sounds like just a comforting *idea* to many of us. How does this new identity shift and shape us everyday? Again, through *words*, but notice what God's words start doing to us.

Those reborn in Christ (John 3) "exhibit a life deriving from an invisible spiritual realm and its powers. . . . Just as with the invisible wind and its effects, we recognize the presence of God's kingdom in a person by its effects in and around them as they progressively become transformed into children of light."[54] That's good, but still a little abstract. What sorts of effects will we have on those around us?

Well, the same effects that the persons indwelling us have! Carrying the candle of God in our chest, the eternal Christ-light, means that we start sharing the *will*, *heart*, and *work* of God. Recall the diagram from the introduction.

THE CHRIST-LIGHT

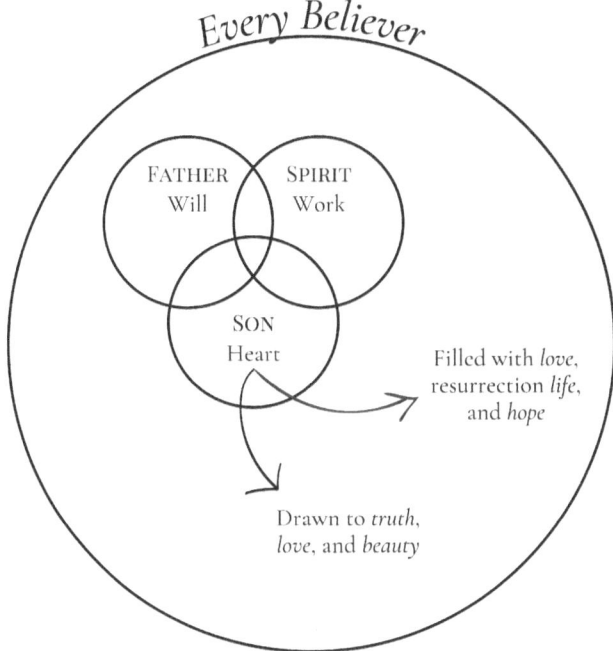

We discover what all of those are in Scripture, of course. Put differently, in Christ we have been given a new life. "Our additional life, though it is still our life, is also God's life in us: his thoughts, his faith, his love, all *literally* imparted to us, shared with us, by his word and Spirit."[55]

We might think of this as *echoed imaging*. We know already that we're image bearers of God—with all the mystery and depth alluded to by that phrase. And yet Paul writes that the Son himself is "the image of the invisible God" (Col. 1:15). Christ said anyone who had seen him had seen his Father (John 14:9). And Christ told the Apostle Paul on the Damascus road that Paul hadn't just been persecuting Christians, but Christ himself (Acts 9:5). It was as if Paul (if he would have been saved earlier in life) should have seen Christ when he looked at Christ's followers. The Son imaged the Father; the children image the Son. Put differently, Jesus said, "Look at me and you'll see God." His followers said, "Look at me and you'll see Christ." Do you see the echoing?

As we read God's word with renewed hearts and minds, the Christ-light grows in us as we start thinking, speaking, and acting more like him—with all of the various facets of his personality. This is what Dallas Willard summarizes as the relationship between consuming God's words and imaging his light.

> A *natural connection* exists between a proper use of the Bible and its ideal result—union with Christ. The Bible expresses the mind of God, since God himself speaks to us through its pages. Thus we, in understanding the Bible, come to share his thoughts and attitudes and even come to share his life through his Word. Scripture is a *communication* that establishes *communion* and opens the way to *union*, all in a way that is perfectly understandable once we begin to have experience of it.[56]

Carrying the Christ-light is a *word journey*. In the words of the gospel, our wicks were relit with the power and purity of God. We can now honor God properly, commune with him deeply, and react to him faithfully. We've become children of light, ushered far from the domain of darkness. Carrying the Christ-light in us each day means that we hear God's words to us in Scripture, prayerfully soaking in the thoughts, attitudes, and works of God in our union with Christ. Our expression of those thoughts, attitudes, and works in the real world is meant to draw others to the Christ-light. We draw nearer to that light by looking through the words of God. We start changing. And the world starts changing.

> By words we grasped a new pulsing heart,
> Casting the dead stone inside us away.
> We burned with a flame only God could impart,
> Turning our shoulders from night into day.
> Now speaking, communing, and growing to one,

We eat divine words as morsels of light.
We feast on God's speech, the words of the Son,
Staring at *him* and eschewing the night.

APPLICATION

Now, that was probably a lot more theology than many readers can handle in one sitting. So let me end the chapter on a more practical note. If this is who we are in Christ, how does it matter to you and me when we wake each morning and fumble down the hallway to the bathroom, trying to rouse our tired selves in a world that already seems to be spinning ahead of us?

Here's how it matters. First, *you are a light-bearer*. The candle of God is in your chest, the Christ-light. Think about that. The God who is everywhere—whose life is brimming and turning in ten thousand starlings, whose calling raises great beasts from the depths of the ocean so they can spray their exhaled mist into the atmosphere, whose words set the billions of stars on fire and keep planets and moons drifting around them, whose breath enters the lungs of every infant pushing through it's mother's body, wet with the blood of giving . . . this God, *this* God has lit the candle inside you. And no one can put it out. Your candle is there to stay.

God must love you *fiercely* to do something so fixed. When you look in the mirror, you can say to that tired reflection staring back,

> The light of Christ is in me,
> Buried beneath all blood and bone.
> I carry what I cannot see
> To my eternal home.

You and I are always fighting spiritual amnesia. We have to work to remember who we are. By God's strange and mysterious providence, through the person of Christ and the power of the Spirit, the world is going to change through *us* (see Rom.

8:18–23). In Murray's words, what God has done and is doing in us through Christ is going to lead to *cosmic regeneration*.[57] *We* are the candles that will set the world aflame, and from its ashes will come a world remade, restored, no longer "groaning" (v. 22) in anticipation of rebirth. But our light won't grow if we keep forgetting who we are. Say it out loud. "I am a light-bearer." Take up some of the threads we explored earlier.

- I am bound in a Christ-secured covenant with God.

- I am bent toward communion with him, carried deeper into union with Christ.

- I am always reacting to what the Spirit shows me about God in his world and word.

We need to rehearse our identity.

Second, when we encounter another brother or sister in Christ, the most fundamental response we must have is to see the Christ-light in them—the God-given, life-leading, irrevocable light. As creatures prone to judge by appearances, this is not intuitive for us. We judge by speech, by clothing, by hair style, by political affiliation, even by beard length (we *are* strange). We judge by anything and everything *except* the God-lit candle in another believer's soul. And the result of our hapless judgment is simple: division. Tribalism and alienation reign in in the church because we don't see what God sees in his own people—the common light of Christ.

This means that every Christ-follower is called to imitate God holistically as they feed on and implement God's words by the Spirit. More specifically, it means all believers live in the same spiritual context: covenant, communion, and reaction. Assuming this truth at the outset would dramatically change how we treat Christians—not as those who oppose us or get in our way, but as creatures who share a gravitational pull toward God, a pull established by their joint union with our Lord. Jesus, as we'll soon witness, was able to see this in his soon-to-be followers, in the darkest of souls. He saw straight through to the Christ-light he would impart—a future home for himself, his Father, and the Spirit. Jesus was always scoping out divine real estate in human souls.

When we don't see that Christ-light in fellow believers, when we refuse to see it, we begin to fill with darkness. Our heads start turning back toward the shadow kingdom because we aren't *seeing* properly. And to see properly is to see the truth of what God has done for his people in Jesus Christ. It was Jesus, after all, who told us to be careful *how* we see. "The eye is the lamp of the body. So, if your eye is healthy, your whole body will be full of light, but if your eye is bad, your whole body will be full of darkness. If then the light in you is darkness, how great is the darkness!" (Matt. 6:22–23).

We're always needing to learn and relearn how to see the Christ-light in our brothers and sisters, how to notice what God set glowing in each human whom he foreknew from eternity. Every Christian needs to keep learning how to be a candle-seeker. And the Spirit will teach us as we continue on our word journey, studying how the light of life can manifest itself in our daily interactions. We'll look at some of those later in the book.

LOTS OF LITTLE LIGHTS

I want to end by pointing out something obvious but constantly ignored about who we are as Christ's light-bearers: we are *limited* and *dependent*—and those are good words, not bad ones.

In his book *You're Only Human*, Kelly Kapic has reminded the people of God that being limited and dependent is not a sin problem; it's a good facet of how God made us. This is especially true for Christians, who know they are only a small part of the body of Christ. "We must learn the value and truthfulness of our finitude, eventually getting to the point where *we might even praise God for our limits*."[58]

Why would he say this? Well, aside from the fact that it's biblical, many Christians have an unhealthy habit of trying to be independent and acting as if we don't need others, as if the little candle in our chest is *all* we really need. This is made worse in the West by a culture that treats independence as a virtue. It's not. Independence is an attribute of God, not of humans. It's something God *is*, not something we should pretend to be. We have, as Kapic put it, a "disordered relationship to our limits."[59]

All this is linked to what we've said about covenant (relationship) and communion. Our limitations, our littleness, propels us toward God and others, and that's how God intended it! "Adam experiences the goodness of creation when he connects his dependence with this other [Eve]. We are designed for communion with each other, and our physicality supplies a medium for that communion. This communion itself exemplifies a kind of need: for God, our neighbors, and the earth."[60]

Each of us in Christ is a little light, looking to link flames with the God of light and with the other little lights around us. Together, we burn brighter. Apart, we dim.

We need to keep this in mind as we think about how to engage with other believers. It affects everything—even the smallest decision to try to move a piece of furniture by ourselves. We constantly need to drop the charade of independence and ask for help. I love how Charlie Mackesy expressed this in a character from his book *The Boy, the Mole, the Fox and the Horse*.

> "What is the bravest thing you've ever said?" asked the boy.
> "Help," said the horse.[61]

Asking for help will serve us well, and it'll save us the back pain, too.

Now that we know who God is and who we are as Christ-light carriers fallen and redeemed, we're ready to stare in wonder at who Jesus is, as the light of God in the flesh. Staring at his light will put us in the perfect position to watch him interact with others. And from there, we'll be able with the Spirit's help to let the truth, love, and beauty of God continue to change us as we meet him in his word.

Reflect

1. How did you understand the image of God before you read this chapter?

2. Which component of the image of God seems hardest for you to accept or apply? Consider the *lex Christi* and also the threads of *covenant*, *communion*, and *reaction*.

3. Select a passage of Scripture to read slowly. As you read it, consider what it reveals to you about how you imitate God. How does the Christ-light inside you enable you to imitate God more faithfully?

Pray

God, you foreknew us in Christ,
As small but strong,
Longing for you and other light-bearers,
Candles leaning on candles.
We came *into* relationship with you,
And we're parched for you now.
Slake our thirst with your Spirit in the word.
Help us see how we're always responding
To what you say about yourself
Within us and outside us.
And help us to see our smallness
As a gift of your greatness.
Let the Christ-light in us grow bolder,
And the domain of darkness fade away.

THE LIGHT OF THE WORLD

If God is the great light above and beyond all earthly lights, then it would be fitting for his Son to share in this motif. And he does, as we've already seen. In the opening of John's Gospel, we read, "In him was life, and the life was the light of men. The light shines in the darkness, and the darkness has not overcome it" (John 1:4–5). A few verses later, John declares, "The true light, which gives light to everyone, was coming into the world" (1:9).

When God enters the world as a human, Light comes to light, the eternal flame to his created candles, those he foreknew before the foundation of the world. And this had (and continues to have) a gloriously dramatic effect on us. As noted in the previous chapter, the coming of Christ is the very thing that lit our wicks, once smoldering and polluting a God-saturated world.

Herman Bavinck, the other Dutch theologian I keep on retainer, summarized the biblical teaching on sin and darkness versus truth and life. Look at the effect the Christ-light has on us.

> When sin pollutes our very being, we hide ourselves, love the darkness, do not dare to show ourselves, and no longer see ourselves as we truly are (Gen. 3:8; John 1:5; 3:19; etc.). Conversely, when through Christ, who is the light (John 1:4–5; 8:12; 9:5; 12:35; 2 Cor. 4:4), God shines in our hearts and gives the light of the knowledge of the glory of God in the face of Jesus Christ (2 Cor. 4:6), we

> regain the courage to look at ourselves, learn to love the light, and again walk in it (Matt. 5:14, 16; John 3:21; Rom. 13:12; Eph. 5:8; Phil. 2:15; 1 Thess. 5:5; 1 John 1:7; etc.).[62]

In Christ, we gain courage to see ourselves, to love the revelation of God, and to imitate him holistically (i.e., faithfully bearing his image).

Bavinck's words also circle around the truth of God's all-encompassing revelation (a key mark of God's covenant). Sin keeps us from *seeing* what God has clearly revealed (i.e., who we really are). And when God shines into our darkened hearts, we receive "the knowledge of the glory of God in the face of Jesus Christ." Remember, as Bavinck wrote, *glory* is another name for *beauty* in Scripture; glory also comes with awe-inspiring light. We receive in Jesus the light and beauty of God—purely based on God's love. In short, the coming of Christ gives us the God of light, with all of his truth, love, and beauty. And it is by his light that we see light (Ps. 36:9).

But Christ's coming doesn't mean a *restoration* of how things used to be, as if we're just trying to get back to the Garden of Eden. Christ's coming is an *advancement*, a going beyond where Adam and Eve were. Christ takes us further; his light casts a longer path in front of us. That's why Geerhardus Vos penned the cryptic words, "Eschatology aims at consummation rather than restoration."[63] What in the world does that mean? It means how things end up will be far better than we first hoped. The light Adam and Eve held in Eden will seem like a shadow compared to the light Christ brings us into (1 Cor. 15:42–49).

THE DISTINGUISHING WORK OF LIGHT

We've talked about God as light and its relationship to truth, love, and beauty. But one of the more fundamental functions of light, linked to truth, is its ability to distinguish one thing from another. That's why getting dressed in a dark closet early in the morning can lead to some strange wardrobe combinations. And this ability of light to distinguish is important to understanding the effect the Christ-light has on us.

Light is actually at the bookends of a Christian worldview. Light was at the beginning of creation, but it's also at the beginning of our re-creation. At the dawn of creation, light was the first thing that God spoke into existence. Reflecting on this, Geerhardus Vos remarked,

> [Light] is prerequisite, not only for the appearance of living beings where it shines, but for all distinguishing and grouping. Light is the image of clarity, of thinking. Consequently, the works of the *Logos* begin with the creation of light. The same connection, the same sequence, between life and light that we meet here we find in the work of re-creation, where regeneration and calling follow each other, just as in creation we see the hovering of the Spirit and the word of power, "Let there be light!"[64]

In creation, light and life follow the divine word. In re-creation, new life and light follow the divine Word.

And this light allows for "distinguishing and grouping." What applies to creation in terms of the different land formations, plants, and animals applies analogously to re-creation in terms of the different traits we acquire in the Spirit (Gal. 5:22). More generally, the Christ-light of re-creation serves to distinguish those who believe from those who don't. Jesus often alluded to this distinguishing feature of light when he spoke of dividing the sheep from the goats (Matt. 25:31–46), or the wheat from the chaff (Matt. 3:12; Luke 3:17). Belief in Christ, the Christ-light, is the basis for distinction.

Contrast, Variation, and Distribution of the Christ-Light

The distinction happens for each believer in unified but diverse ways. The linguist I studied, Kenneth L. Pike, often wrote about units of language as having three different types of information: *contrast, variation,* and *distribution*.[65] We can apply these concepts not just to human identity in general, but to our possession of the Christ-light. I promise this will be painless and far less academic than it sounds.

Contrast. Each of us possesses the Christ-light as a unique creature of God, with a personality and history that contrasts with those of others. Christ redeems all of us from the domain of darkness, but he redeems each one of us as individuals—with our unique patterns of sin and disbelief. Yet, he redeems us not so that we can be separate from each other, but so that we can join together in the body of Christ as a testament to his vast work of redemption. The diversity of our redemption serves the unity of Christ's church. I say this because *you are a light-bearer like no other, and yet you belong with other light-bearers.*

Variation. Second, each day, we wake up the same . . . and yet slightly different. I wake up with fewer hairs on my head and more wrinkles under my eyes, but there are plenty of other changes, too. By God's grace, I'm learning more about how I can be the person Christ has called me to be. I make plenty of mistakes each day, but I'm inching toward Christ-likeness one moment at a time—in the attention I give to someone else, in the way I hold my tongue when a rash judgment wants to jump out, in the patience that speaks through silence. Each day I am a new variant of myself, clinging to that same Christ-light, but watching it work on me differently hour by hour. I say this because *you are a light-bearer who is still growing and changing.*

Distribution. As carriers of the Christ-light, each of us fits into a series of "slots" each day, in our various relationships. We are husbands, brothers, co-workers, sons, fathers, cousins, grandchildren, artists, writers, landscapers, teachers, businessmen, real estate agents, and so on. Carrying the Christ-light matters in each of these slots. We can be tempted to compartmentalize our faith and only think of ourselves as followers of Christ in a few areas. But that's not what we're called to in the Spirit. We're called to carry the Christ-light everywhere we go, into every relationship. I say this because *you are a light-bearer in every area of life*.

This is how each one of us possesses and grows in our reception and application of the Christ-light. You can see how Christ changes everything.

What Christ as Light Did for Us

Christ, of course, is responsible for distinguishing us with his light, for setting us apart so that we could possess his aura as unique creatures, growing and changing in every facet of life. This required a grand sacrifice, a giving of the Christ-candle for each of us. Christ went down to the dark of death, where every wick is cold and wet, and he went to pour out what was inside himself—blood—in order to heal *our* insides. The life in Christ's blood bore light in our souls. He took what is bitter so we could taste what is sweet. As Herbert wrote in his poem "The Agony,"

> Love is that liquor sweet and most divine,
> Which my God feels as blood; but I as wine.

We could rewrite the couplet with the theme of light.

> Love is that holy light of God among men,
> Which cost him darkness, but gave breath again.

What amazes me is that God would have been fully within his covenantal rights to come down from heaven as a blazing fire, burning up all who opposed him, obliterating every creaturely candle corrupting the world with its smoke trail. And yet instead he came to ignite us; he came to illuminate and enliven, to save the very ones destroying the created world he spoke into being.

He came to set apart those who had already put themselves on the wrong side.

And this would have been beyond grace on its own, but God went even further. He *died* to take away our death. He let himself go dim so that we might cling to the risen Christ and glow. Why did he do this? Once more, the only answer we have is the mystery of divine love, the sovereign will of a loving God. He *willed* to do this. He *willed* to restore the covenant, bring communion, and help us react to his truth. He *willed* our oneness. As Paul Miller wrote, "Jesus died to bring people *together and make them one*. The goal of his love is oneness.... Jesus finds joy in restoring people to the sanity of a God-centered life."[66] And when we have the Christ-light, when we live God-centered lives—as unique creatures, growing in the Spirit, in every facet of life—we can glow with the glory of God, drawing other eyes to see the wonder of God.

Christ as the Light of Life

Christ as the light is also the origin of life. Just as God's light in Genesis led to life in the beginning of time, so the person of light (John 8:12) leads to life at the end of times. The light is the only thing that can save a soul closed in by rebellious walls of darkness. He says plainly, "I am the light of the world. Whoever follows me will not walk in darkness, but will have the light of life" (John 8:12).

Home in on that phrase, "the light of life." What does it mean to have this? John Calvin says that through Christ as the light "the brightness of the divine glory is made known to me n."[67] The brightness of divine glory—the light of God himself. And that brings us back once more to truth, love, and beauty.

To have the "light of life" in Christ is to live in God's country, a land illuminated by his own nature. In Christ, we're drawn to the truth, repelling falsehood. In Christ, we're moved to love—to affirm the Christ-light in other believers and give ourselves to them. In Christ, we're gripped by beauty. Each of these terms (truth, love, and beauty) can serve as perspectives on each other. Let's end the chapter by looking through the lens of beauty.

The poet David Whyte said, "beauty is the conversation between what we think is happening outside in the world and what is just about to occur far inside us."[68] He continues, "Beauty is an achieved state of both deep attention and self-forgetting."[69] The light *outside* of us in Christ becomes the light *inside* of us by the Spirit. That's beauty.

But I say that beauty isn't an "achieved state." It's a divine person. It's Jesus Christ, the Son of God, Light of Light, the person of truth and love. And yes, when we meet him, he draws out both our deep attention and self-forgetting. Having the light of life in Christ means that our jaws drop at the radiance of God at the same time that we forget ourselves. These two components—awe and self-forgetfulness—are going to be critical when it comes to seeing the Christ-light in other believers. And it's in Jesus's interactions with others that this comes to the fore. That's where we turn now.

REFLECT

1. What does it mean to you when you hear that Christ is the "light of the world"?

2. How does receiving the light of Christ change us (think of contrast, variation, and distribution)?

3. Why do you think Scripture uses the language of "light" for God and love, and "darkness" for sin and death?

PRAY

Jesus, my light and my love,
You came to me,
And you took my darkness.

You wrapped yourself in it,
And brought it down to death,
Where you tore it to pieces
With the everlasting light of love.
Thank you for ripping apart
What kept me from you.
Thank you for glowing in me,
For making your light my light.
Please, Lord, help me see how your light
Has the power to brighten all of your people.

THE LIGHT IN THE WORLD

WE'VE LOOKED AT WHAT the Christ-light is, stepped back to stare at the God of light (truth, love, and beauty), stepped closer to see how creatures of light fell and were restored, and then gazed at the light of the world and his distinguishing work in us.

Now, knowing all of this, I want you to read a passage with fresh eyes. It's a passage that never ceases to amaze me. It was the very passage, in fact, that God used to encourage me to write this book. Read it slowly now, keeping in mind what we've seen about who God is (the Father of lights), who we are in Christ (light-bearers), and who Christ is (the true light of the world who gave himself for us). Here's how the light of the world chooses to interact with the lost.

> And as Jesus reclined at table in the house, behold, many tax collectors and sinners came and were reclining with Jesus and his disciples. And when the Pharisees saw this, they said to his disciples, "Why does your teacher eat with tax collectors and sinners?" But when he heard it, he said, "Those who are well have no need of a physician, but those who are sick. Go and learn what this means: 'I desire mercy, and not sacrifice.' For I came not to call the righteous, but sinners." (Matt. 9:10–13; Mark 2:16–17; Luke 5:29–32)

This is one of the many passages where the glory of the gospel shows how blind we are, how darkness walls us in, how we *need* the light of God to come for us.

We need to know a few things to have this passage strike us. First, the sharing of a meal in Jesus's culture wasn't just a casual get-together. Those you ate with were those to whom you bound yourself. Your dinner companions were your deepest connections.

> In ancient Israel the table was a place where spiritual points were taught and where fellowship occurred. The term "dinner" often connotes a banquet (a festive meal where people reclined), which was probably in Jesus's honor. Eating with someone established a covenant relationship of friendship, which normally also signified approval. In one ancient story, two warriors stopped fighting each other when they discovered that their fathers had shared a meal! The issue of eating with sinners was sensitive in Judaism since some believed that eating with such company conveyed acceptance of that person's sin. Jesus preferred pursuing relationships that might lead sinners to God rather than "quarantining" himself from such people.[70]

Jesus, the light of God, the light of the world, is holding fellowship with doused and fuming wicks. Why? There's something truly beautiful about knowing that the only answer to this question is *the mystery of love*.

THE POWER OF LOVE'S MYSTERY

We constantly search for reasons, for the *whys* of our behavior. But love goes deeper than reason. If I asked my wife to tell me *why* she loves me, she's kind and gracious enough to come up with a list of reasons to help me feel better about myself. But while that might be appealing to me in the moment, it wouldn't satisfy in the long run. My confidence would fade. Why? Because I would start to doubt the traits she listed or worry that one day I wouldn't possess them. Would she love me less in that case? How many attractive traits would I need to maintain to secure her love? You can sense the deep danger of this game, can't you?

In contrast, if I asked my wife why she loved me and she said, "I just do," I might not get the ego boost I wanted, but that answer would end up satisfying me in the depths of my soul. Why? Because it goes beyond reason and explanation. It's hidden in the mystery of her own *will*. And so there's no list of traits for me to maintain. All I have to do is be myself—as challenging as that can be in a world where we always stare at the accomplishments of others. I don't have to work for her affection. I don't have to maintain her docket of reasons for loving me, adding something to the list if one trait weakens or disappears. Instead—and this part is critical—I *want* to love her with all of myself in response. I'm motivated to love her from my heart, not from a sense of anxiety or ego protection.

Something analogous happens with the love of God, the love of Christ that seeks out sinners and sufferers. It goes beyond reason, beyond explanation. When we think about it, that isn't so strange, since the most mysterious and beautiful being is God, and God *is* love (1 John 4:8). Bavinck wrote that love "is independent, eternal, and unchangeable, like God himself."[71] We can no more explain love than we can expound on the depths of God. There's no getting around the mystery. There is no "God loves us *because* . . ."

There's great power in this because the power comes from *God* and not from *us* (cf. 2 Cor. 4:7–9). If we could come up with a reason for why God loves us, it wouldn't be a very good reason. It would be brittle. Time would fade it. Our sin would fracture it. But when the only reason for God's love is hidden in the mystery of his will, that reason cannot be touched. It's safe, guarded, and constantly drawing gratitude and awe. This is as it should be, because the love God has for us is a reflection of the love he has for himself among Father, Son, and Spirit. How could we ever fathom that love? Vern Poythress wrote, "The love of God comes through reflection, which has its archetype in the Son, who is the eternal Image or reflection of God the Father. The love of God in the world reflects the eternal love of the Father for the Son (John 3:35). God's Trinitarian love is unfathomable."[72] And praise God that it *is* unfathomable. What we can fathom will fade; mystery forever blooms.

That forever-blooming mystery is what walks into a room full of sinners in Matthew 9. And while the mystery of divine love is the only reason we can give for Jesus's communing with these darkened souls, we can say a bit more about the appropriateness of this crowd as compared to self-righteous religious elites.

TO JOIN THE KINGDOM

Jesus reclined at table with the outcasts as those who had no delusions about who they were. Everyone else was still hoodwinked by some trick of the devil into thinking that they were okay on their own. But these tax collectors and sinners knew who they were and what they needed.

What did they need? *Not* what those around them claimed to have—a righteousness of their own. God's kingdom of light required more. As Bavinck had it, what we need to participate in God's kingdom

> is not a righteousness of one's own but repentance (*metanoia*), a change of mind, and faith (*pistis*), the acceptance of and trust in the gospel of the kingdom as God's gift to the lost (Mark 1:15), and therefore trust in God (Mark 11:22), in Jesus's word and power (Matt. 8:10; 9:2; Mark 4:40), in Jesus as the Messiah (Matt. 27:42; Mark 9:42; John 1:12; 2:11; 6:29; 17:8; 20:31; Acts 9:22; 17:3; 18:5; etc.). But even this *metanoia* and *pistis* themselves are again gifts of God's grace (Matt. 11:25, 27;

15:13; 16:17; Luke 10:22; John 6:44, 65; 12:32).[73]

What grants you entrance into the kingdom of light? What opens the darkened chambers of your soul so that you can receive the aura of God's Son—taking on the will, heart, and work of God himself? An *admission* that you need help and *faith* in the one who can give it. And yet even here, Bavinck notes that this admission and the faith accompanying it are *gifts*. So we're pushed once more back to the mysterious love of God, who enabled the tax collectors and sinners to offer both of these things. In God's providence, the religious leaders weren't. The Spirit of the loving God had not moved their hearts to admission and faith. And so they remained doused and fuming candle wicks, still under the impression that they didn't need divine help to become righteous, that change wasn't a God-given gift. Their minds remained stuck in what John Murray called *a delirium of vanity*.

AWE AND SELF-FORGETFULNESS

Our marvel at Matthew 9:10–13 should be in this: Jesus approaches the *darkest* of souls—those who not only let off no light but who also were poisoning the lives around them—and he ignites them with love so that they might brighten the world with the Christ-light. He makes night day and shadow light. He turns poisonous wicks of the world into candles glowing for God. He does all this through a faith that the Spirit himself gives, the Spirit of Christ (Rom. 8:11). This is nothing short of miraculous. It's worth our *awe*.

In fact, true faith rising up in God's people is even worth awe on the part of *Christ*. Remember that having the light of life, the Christ-light, means letting our jaws drop at the radiance of God as we forget ourselves.

Jesus even does this, as the very light of God incarnate! What does he do in the presence of Spirit-given faith? When he encounters a centurion whose faith in words mirrors what's needed for receiving the gospel, he *marvels*. "Truly," he says, "I tell you, with no one in Israel have I found such faith" (Matt. 8:10). The centurion's faith is worth marveling at because it's a gift of God himself (Eph. 2:8), and all of God's gifts are worth our awe and attention. The centurion believed in Jesus, as is evident by his request. He thus had the light of life given to him by the Spirit, and so Jesus marvels. He marvels that this man, standing *outside* the nation of Israel, is more than ready to begin his *word journey*, to receive the Christ-light, since he's already understood the power of words that leads to life. Marvel. Awe. That's the first response we have to the light of life, the Christ-light who saves.

The second is *self-forgetfulness*. Jesus does this for his whole life in a way we can't fathom. For even his coming here, to this humble planet, was an act of self-forgetfulness, of putting his Father's will and the salvation of souls above himself. The passage focusing on this is Philippians 2:5–8.

> Have this mind among yourselves, which is yours in Christ Jesus, who, though he was in the form of God, did not count equality with God a thing to be grasped, but emptied himself, by taking the form of a servant, being born in the likeness of men. And being found in human form, he humbled himself by becoming obedient to the point of death, even death on a cross.

For Jesus to hold onto himself would be to grasp equality with God. And that was his right, his heritage. But he didn't count that equality with God as something to *grasp*; he counted it as something to *give*—not that we could become equal with God but that all that separates us from God (sin) might be removed. Jesus's divine self-forgetfulness is what extends the light of life to all of us. He forgot himself so that God could eternally remember us.

What's our response to the Christ-light? A corresponding awe and self-forgetfulness. That is what the centurion displays.

He has an awe-struck faith in God's power, matched by a sort of self-forgetfulness. He asks, after all, for his *servant* to be healed, not for something selfish.

All of this tempers our understanding of what Jesus was doing in Matthew 9:10–13. Jesus is the great light dawning in our darkness and death (Matt. 4:16). He comes to a world of doused and fuming candles, and he gives us the light of life; he gives us *himself*. The light *of* the world came to make us lights *in* the world. Christ is our illumination. He puts *his* light inside us, and he never takes it back. He sets us free to chase after truth, love, and beauty. And he does so knowing that we now possess the will, heart, and work of the God who lives inside us.

I don't tend to see other Christians this way, as light-bearers. In fact, I don't tend to see *myself* this way. I stare at the darkness in me, my indwelling sin, and I stare at the darkness in other believers. Even as I wrote these words, I found that my wife was being attacked on social media by another Christian because she shops at a certain store. I thought, "How petty! And how hypocritical! I mean, what does this person think the social media platform *she's* using supports? Orphans and widows? I doubt it. God, it makes me embarrassed to be a human!" I saw the darkness in a stranger. It was *so* obvious.

But what about the Christ-light? Why didn't I see that? Probably because I wasn't looking for it. Remember that we're called to discipline not just *what* we see but *how* we see. Of course, I also didn't see it because Christians are inconsistent. We have the Christ-light within us, but we don't always live in ways that draw attention to it. We don't always point to the truth, love, and beauty of God. In fact, sometimes we live in ways that resemble our dead selves from the shadow kingdom.

The difference in our engagement with fellow believers is a matter of *seeing*, of *looking*. Paul Miller once wrote, "Love begins with looking."[74] It begins by sympathizing with others, by seeing the world from their perspective. "To be lovers of people, we need to look at them. Like Jesus we must see them. Like him, we must stop, look, and listen."[75] But more specifically for Christians, we must stop and stare at the Christ-light, no matter how shrouded it may be by indwelling sin. Christ came for *this* person. Christ died for *this* person. Christ rose from the grave for *this* person. Christ dwells in *this* person. If we look for the Christ-light in our brothers and sisters, we will find it. Because it's there. Asking a few questions and being patient to listen will reveal that they, too, want to follow God's will, have the heart of Christ, and are working by the Spirit.

So, what if I had chosen instead to just *look* at this woman who lashed out on social media, to pray in the Spirit about how I could encourage this person's growth? Wouldn't that be more helpful than an angry rant? Wouldn't that be more faithful to the heart of Christ, the light of the world?

This is just one example of thousands I could pull from. I want to get better at following Jesus. I want to do what he does. I want to see the light in his people, those chosen in him before a fleck or fiber of the cosmos came into being. And I want to know how I can work in the Spirit to draw that light out, in testament to the light-giving Lord who governs my life. This drawing out of light, after all, is what Jesus has done for each of us. It's in remembrance of the joy of our salvation that we chase Jesus's footsteps.

How Jesus Interacts

As part of my research for this book, I read slowly through the four gospels with one question in mind: *how does Jesus interact with people?* I knew at this point that passages such as Matthew 9:10–13 were "the most magnificent proof of God's compassion."[76] But what sparked my curiosity was *how* this way of looking at God's people affected Jesus's interactions—what he said, what he did, the way he taught. In other words, how does looking for the Christ-light in our brothers and sisters change how we respond to them when they're sick, or irritating, or judgmental, or self-righteous. And does it make a positive difference in how we approach fellow believers when nothing is wrong?

This is where much of the book will now focus. And, as you can imagine, I found great variety in Jesus's conversations with lepers and lame men, blind beggars and barbarous bigots—even with his own family members. While I can't convey all that I found, my goal is to paint a portrait with as many colors as I can. We'll be able to recognize these colors in the canvas of our own daily life and take some steps toward imaging Jesus more faithfully. Here's where we'll focus for the remainder.

- Seeing as a Servant
- Seeing the Sheep
- Unveiling the Light with Questions
- Seeing Light by Telling Stories
- Unrestricted Forgiveness
- What Brightening Looks Like
- Love and Giving

REFLECT

1. In what ways was Jesus a "light" to those he encountered?

2. Why do you think we tend to shun people who have sinned, even other believers, removing ourselves from them, as the Pharisees did from the "tax collectors and sinners"?

3. In what ways does God's giving of the Christ-light bring you to marvel? In what ways has it led to self-forgetfulness?

PRAY

Jesus, you saw things I have trouble seeing.
You went toward those we run from,
Touching the untouchable,
Healing the unhealable,
Covering the dark of sin with the light of forgiveness.
Work in us, by your Spirit,
To help us see your light in our brothers and sisters,
The light that *you* gave.
And show us, one conversation at a time,
How we might brighten it in your honor.

SEEING AS A SERVANT

Jesus Christ sees the light he put inside us. But that means that he sees us *in a certain way*. There is always a *way* of seeing, a vantage point, a perspective. And this way shapes what we think of others and how we respond to them. The *way* shapes the *what*. The *looking* leads to *love*. This is where we ended the last chapter.

Jesus had every right to come as a sovereign, to sweep humanity into piles like dust mites and judge the faithless and the godless on the spot. But he didn't.

Jesus had every right to come as a religious elite, showing how perfectly he fulfilled every letter of the law and how double-minded the rest of us are. But he didn't.

Jesus had every right to come as a political ruler, showing the whole world what an earthly king *should* be. But he didn't.

Jesus came as a *servant*. He told his closest friends, "whoever would be great among you must be your servant, and whoever would be first among you must be slave of all. For even the Son of man came not to be served but to serve, and to give his life as a ransom for many" (Mark 10:43–45). Christ came to *serve* and *give*. This is the light of the world we're talking about, the spinner of galaxies, the commander of ten billion angels, who silences storms with a word and restores bodies with a touch. *This* one came to serve and give. That is his primary objective as he brings the light of God to those whom God foreknew (Rom. 8:29). Because of this, servants are kings in Christ's court. We are highest when we are lowest. We are tallest when we bow down. We burn brightest when our hands are open.

Service and self-giving are perhaps the clearest earmarks of Jesus's life. Whenever he's engaging with others, there's always some sense in which he's serving or giving. But how do serving and giving ignite the wick inside God's people? Why has God chosen to act in *this* way so that the Spirit kindles the flame of faith in us?

Let me use an analogy. How do you get a plant to grow? You know you can't force a sprout from the soil or squeeze a tree from an acorn. Growth does not come by force. The seed grows by being served. It responds *internally* to what we do for it *externally*. If a seed is going to germinate and take root, change must work from the inside out, not from the outside in. The same applies to human souls. We need renovation from the inside out. Christ brings light *inside* to effect change on the *outside*. By the breath of God's own Spirit, the Christ-light ignites our wick. That inner, God-given light grows as the Spirit keeps working in us, bringing about change and growth, light and warmth, spiritual beauty.

The internal change ripples outward. The Christ-light inside us doesn't just brighten us; it brightens the rest of God's people. When Jesus serves and gives himself to others, did you ever notice what happens? Those people turn and start serving and giving. It becomes a divine ripple of blessing, a wave of light moving through the dim world. Jesus heals Simon's mother-in-law from a fever. What does she do? She immediately begins serving them (Mark 1:29–31). Jesus washes his disciples' feet and then calls them into the footwashing enterprise (John 13:14). He tells story after story of how grace, mercy, and forgiveness (services of God) are meant to be passed on (Matt. 18:21–22; 18:33; Mark 5:19; 11:25; Luke 22:26–27). He tells us to believe in the light. Why? "That you may become sons of light" (John 12:36). And sons of light shine for others (Matt. 5:16). Redemption is a wave of light that rolls over us but also carries us in its current. What God does for us we are meant to do for others.

Christ sees God's people with this serving and self-giving perspective. He sees the doused and fuming candle in a fallen human heart and says, "I come to give the light of love."

APPLICATION

Is that how you see other believers, as a servant looking for chances to give? Is that how I see them? Honesty is the first step toward healing. We typically do the opposite, don't we? We approach others by tacitly asking, "How can this person serve me? What can I get from him?" This happens across relationships—co-workers, friends, family members, spouses. We know we should aim to serve and hope to give, but we aim to take and hope to receive. How does God's Spirit save us from this? How does the Christ-light burn away our selfish old self?

In short, God gives us everything. And then he asks, "Now what?" Paul says that in Christ we've been given "every spiritual blessing" (Eph. 1:3). He says in his second letter to the Corinthians that we possess *everything* (2 Cor. 6:10). In his letter to the Colossians he says we have been *filled* by Christ (Col. 2:10), the one who is full of the very light of God. We are more than rich; we possess every good thing imaginable. We have more gifts than we can count, more riches than any king or corporate billionaire. In Jesus Christ and by the Spirit, we are inheritors of the greatest wealth: the promises of God (Heb. 6:12).

So, put the question to yourself. "Now what?" If you truly believe you possess all things in Christ, you won't be looking for what you can get from others and how they can serve you. It will be the opposite. Christ knew with the certainty of God who he was and what kingdom belonged to his Father. In that sure knowledge, he came to serve and to give. The certainty of his identity and inheritance laid the foundation for his engagement with others. The same is meant to apply to us as co-heirs with Christ (Rom. 8:17). And while possessing "every spiritual blessing" and "everything" in Christ seems overwhelming, it gets better. What's implied in Romans 8:17 is that "God himself is the inheritance of his children (cf. Ps. 73:25, 26; Lam. 3:24)."[77] Christ inherits the glorious light who *is* his heavenly Father. As joint heirs, we inherit *God*, not merely spiritual blessings or the things that God has made. It's *him*. He's the soul-satisfying

Father of lights we long for, the one Jesus prays for us to be one with (John 17:21).

Is that enough? Really—is it enough? Because if it isn't, we're going to keep seeking what other people can give us.

Seeing the Christ-light in our brothers and sisters is a matter of deeply believing in God's promises to us. We think that trying harder is the key to seeing the best in others, to serving and giving. But that leads to failure and guilt. To see the Christ-light that God's own Spirit has ignited in his people, we must stare at the gift of God that Christ gave. Only when we see our own riches will we be in a position to serve and give ourselves to others. Seeing as a servant means staring at our savior and then turning to give from his glorious wealth.

So, that's where we start. Light-bearers are called to the Christ-light in others, which includes their covenantal, communion-seeking, ever-reacting personality. To see and praise God for the Christ-light in our faith family, we follow in Christ's footsteps by seeing *as* a servant. This is a way of seeing that takes time and prayer to practice. And it takes continual reminders from God's word that we are already truly and eternally rich. It's from faith in that word that we can kneel before others seeking to serve and give.

Yet what does this serving and giving look like, and how, practically, can we draw attention to the light in others? That's where we go in the following chapters. But first, we need one more discussion on how Jesus saw people—not just as his light-bearers but as lost sheep. Seeing others as wandering sheep changes how we might engage with them.

REFLECT

1. What are some of the ways Christ saw others as a servant? How did they respond to his servitude?

2. What keeps us from seeing as servants? What are the competing vantage points we have inside us?

3. It can be hard for some of us to *be served*. We want to be the one always serving and giving. How is rejecting the service of others problematic in the kingdom of God?

PRAY

Jesus, you came from above but saw us from below.
You looked up at us from the dust,
As a servant and a giver.
You offered.
You taught.
You healed.
You prayed.
You gave *all* for us,
Serving as King
A populace of paupers.
Brighten us in the Spirit.
Grow and glow our hearts
So that our hands open to give,
Or gather dirt from foot washing.

SEEING THE SHEEP

IN THE LAST CHAPTER, we learned that Jesus saw God's people in a certain way and calls us, by his Spirit, to do the same. And while it's true that he approached them as a servant, he also knew where they were before he found them: *lost*. No one wants that word to describe himself, but it's true—before Christ found us and even after that when we stray off the path. We get lost. It's this lostness that Jesus recognizes in all the crowds that followed him. And when people were "found" by him, they didn't respond in the ways we might think. But let's start with sheep.

NEEDY, VULNERABLE, AND MISGUIDED

As the crowds followed Jesus from town to town, deserted place to deserted place, mountainside to lakeshore, Jesus had compassion on them. Why? "Because they were harassed and helpless, like sheep without a shepherd" (Matt. 9:36).

Sheep without a shepherd are *needy*, *vulnerable*, and *misguided*. That's *everyone* apart from Christ.

Needy. Sheep are needy for lots of reasons, but one of the biggest ministries Jesus offered was *healing*. Early in Luke's Gospel, we read, "Now when the sun was setting, all those who had any who were sick with various diseases brought them to him, and he laid his hands on every one of them and healed them" (Luke 4:40). I love that Luke uses the expression "every one of them." Every. Single. One. The lame and the lepers, the blind and the broken, the feverish and the frail—he healed them *all*. They needed that.

But beneath these physical needs were the more pronounced and vital spiritual needs. As a kid, I always found it strange that Jesus forgave sins as a response to those looking for healing, as with the paralytic. Here's a man who can't even put his two feet on the ground, and what does Jesus say? "Take heart, my son; your sins are forgiven" (Matt. 9:2; Mark 2:5). Jesus looked at this paralyzed man and knew that the greatest threat to him was not a broken body but a broken heart, a doused and fuming wick that needed the Christ-light. Bodies will eventually break down. Limbs will weaken. Joints will stiffen. Though our souls are immortal, these bodies aren't. What is of utmost importance for this man? What will Jesus do to truly help him? Heart healing. In other words, Jesus is going to light his soul's candle, to set fire where darkness dwelled. His light, his person, is of *eternal* importance.

Jesus had to repeat this message often. People had trouble seeing what he was trying to give them. After being trailed by crowds for multiplying loaves of bread, Jesus levels with them. "You are seeking me, not because you saw signs, but because you ate your fill of the loaves" (John 6:26).

We have this problem, just as the crowds did: we chase after things that don't last. Bread. Alcohol. Clothes. Cruises. Money. Accolades. Our list of perishable passions goes on. Perishable passions don't require faith. They just require feelings, and we all have those. But Jesus is very clear: those will not satisfy us. And how could they, if we're creatures longing not for commodities but for communion? "Do not work for the food that perishes, but for the food that endures to eternal life, which the Son of man will give to you" (John 6:27). Jesus sees our true *need*. And he meets it with *himself*. He does that for every wandering sheep in the fold of God.

Vulnerable. Jesus also saw the vulnerability of God's people. Why? Staying with Jesus's concern for human hearts, it wasn't just physical threats he had in mind—though physical threats certainly have an effect on our heart. The people were vulnerable to false teaching. "Beware the teaching of the Pharisees," he would say (Matt. 16:6, 11; Mark 8:15; Luke 12). Why should they beware? Because the people were surrounded by hypocrites (Luke 12:1). They were surrounded by leaders who encouraged them to harp on the law and "good" works to the detriment of other people.

The story of the good Samaritan focuses on this (Luke 10:25–37). The two men who walked past the beaten one were holy—a priest and a Levite. Touching the beaten man on the side of the road would have made them unclean. In fact, he may have been presumed dead, and they could not touch a dead thing (Num. 19:13). The law trumped careful compassion. Appearances were safer than sincerity. And it was no accident that the righteous one in this parable is an outsider, someone beyond the walled gates of the holy Jewish community. Jesus is highlighting the wickedness of hypocrisy, of claiming to follow and worship the God of compassion and loving-kindness while discarding the image bearers of that God as secondary to the keeping of a moral code.

Hypocrisy is ugly. But it's also misleading and influential for vulnerable people. It suggests that the outside is more important than the inside, and that is inimical to Jesus's very life and ministry. "Woe to you," Jesus tells the Pharisees, "for you are like white-washed tombs, which outwardly appear beautiful, but within are full of dead people's bones and all uncleanness" (Matt. 23:27). Do you see the irony? In striving for ceremonial cleanliness, the Pharisees' hypocrisy makes them unclean. They *appear* to be living for God, but really they're just dead (doused and fuming wicks). And yet their hypocrisy was leading people away from God, because sheep are vulnerable. They have needs, and they bite at anything that might satisfy. They long to be righteous, since they're covenant creatures longing for communion with a holy God. But a superficial holiness looks just as appetizing (maybe even more so!) than true humility and self-sacrifice—the hallmarks of Christ's holiness. The sheep are needy, but they're also vulnerable to false teaching.

Misguided. Lastly, the sheep are misguided. They don't know where they're going or how they'll get there. And in one of the most beautiful images, Jesus tells them what they need: a voice. "My sheep hear my voice, and I know them, and they follow me" (John 10:27). Sheep don't need better *sight* to go in the right direction; they need better *hearing*. And Jesus is the good shepherd with a beautiful voice (John 10:11). The sheep of two thousand years ago and of today need to hear the voice of Christ. Apart from that, they will wander.

Jesus has compassion on God's people because they're like sheep without a shepherd. They're needy, vulnerable, and misguided. Jesus alone provides what they need by offering himself. He is the bread that forever fills (John 6:48–51). Jesus alone offers the restoration of hearts and unending communion with the Father through the Spirit. Jesus alone guides his people with the truth as they listen to the sound of his voice. That voice is the voice of love, which is self-giving. "Greater love has no one than this, that someone lay down his life for his friends" (John 15:13). That is how people will identify us as his sheep, as followers of the good shepherd: not by our doctrine or by our morality or our self-righteousness, but by our *love* (John 13:35).[78]

APPLICATION

Seeing as a servant means we recognize ourselves and the rest of God's people as sheep: needy, vulnerable, and misguided. What applied to God's people in Jesus's day still applies to us today. All the Christians we encounter, including ourselves, are struggling or completely failing at seeing how desperately they need Jesus, how central the Christ-light is to their well-being and direction, how only one voice can lead them where they need to go. We don't often see ourselves and others this way because everyone wears a cloak of independence. But one puff of wind blows it off and reveals just how dependent we are on the garments of mercy and grace by a tailoring transcendence.

If we don't see God's people as sheep, will we have the impetus to serve and give ourselves to them? The urgency fades when we think fellow believers are "mostly okay." They're okay in the sense that the Christ-light dwells in them and they cannot be taken from his hand. But they're still sheep. They still need a shepherd. When they wander, they're threatened.

I'll end with a common example. How often do we hear believers respond this way to our offer to pray for them? "No, that's okay. I'm good." I always smile when I hear that because I think, "Do we live in the same world?" Of course, there's nothing wrong with being "good" or content in Christ. We should strive for that! But we're all in process by the Spirit. We're all still sheep wandering on the hills, fighting to follow the good voice. Why don't we approach other believers that way? Why don't we search for opportunities to point to Christ when we see a need, vulnerability, or search for direction? I'm making things simpler than they are, I know. But the fundamental point still holds. We need to approach every one of God's people as a sheep longing for Christ's voice, no matter how many times they serve up the "No thanks; I'm good." There is more beneath the surface if we're willing to wait and listen. Our problem is that we usually aren't.

We need listening practice, and listening is an active, immersive behavior. It's a giving of silence. And it requires all of us. Adam S. McHugh wrote,

> Listening is never passive, a stall or placeholder until doing steps in and saves the day. Biblical listening is a whole-hearted, full-bodied listening that not only vibrates our eardrums but echoes in our souls and resonates into our limbs. John's famous picture of Jesus as the Word of God means that Jesus's entire incarnated life, not only his parables and sermons, is the expression of God's mind. His life is God's speech to us. We are correspondingly asked to listen with our lives, and we are not truly listening unless we are responding to Jesus with all our heart, mind, soul, and strength.[79]

Listening—pure and simple—is a lost art. And we need it

back if we're going to see the Christ-light in our brothers and sisters, to see as a servant, to see them as sheep in constant and unfading need of Christ. Listening, as with looking, will be key.

The next chapter gets into one concrete method of entering into this sort of listening.

REFLECT

1. If we're not thinking of God's people as sheep, how are we thinking of them? What images come to mind?

2. How do you think the Pharisees saw themselves in Jesus's day? Are there parallels in your own life?

3. What are some ways that you feel needy, vulnerable, and misguided? How does Christ meet you in these areas? Ask for prayer from a brother or sister.

PRAY

> Jesus, our shepherd true and steady,
> We are your sheep—
> Needy, vulnerable, misguided.
> But you call us back.
> You call us to yourself.
> Only you can satisfy.
> Only you can protect us with the truth.
> Only you can lead us in the way everlasting.
> Help us to notice when our feet
> Are stepping off the path
> You have pressed into the grass for us.
> Help us to see others as sheep.
> Give us great compassion.
> And help us point them to you.

UNVEILING THE LIGHT WITH QUESTIONS

AN IMPORTANT PART OF listening well is learning to ask good questions. But what makes a question "good"? We have to expand our understanding if we want to see how Jesus uses words to illuminate God's people. While he does this in many ways, we'll focus on *questions* because they are an easy tool at our disposal each day.

JESUS'S QUESTIONS

Here's my favorite fact about Jesus's questions: He already knows the answer to every single one! Sit on that truth for a few minutes. We're so used to questions only being used to elicit information that we think Jesus must be doing the same—or at least going through the motions for our sake. But everything Jesus does, everything *God* does, is done with poetic intentionality.

My favorites are when Jesus asks obvious questions. He asks two blind men, "What do you want me to do for you?" (Matt. 20:32). He asks a lame man, "Do you want to be healed?" (John 5:6). He asks Philip where they're going to buy bread right before he multiplies the loaves and feeds five thousand (John 6:5). He asks a weeping Mary at his own tomb, "Whom are you seeking?" (John 20:15). Why is he doing this?

The short answer: Jesus's questions aren't for him; they're for us. Do you ever notice the *effect* these questions have on us? They help us to do two things: *confess* and *notice*. We can also tie these actions to the truth, love, and beauty of God. We confess the truth, notice how the love of God meets us, and fall into the beauty of grace all over again.

Confession seems simple and short. We pass over its glory in search of the "real" work of repentance. But confession *is* real work. It does things inside us.

The poet I quoted earlier, David Whyte, once wrote,

> Confession is a stripping away of protection, the telling of a truth which might once have seemed like a humiliation, become suddenly a gateway, an entrance to solid ground; even a first step home. To confess is to free oneself, not only by admitting a sin or an omission but to profess a deeper allegiance, a greater dedication to something beyond the mere threat of immediate punishment or the desolation of being shunned. To confess is to declare oneself ready for a more courageous road, one in which a previously defended identity might not only be shorn away, but be seen to be irrelevant, a distraction, a working delusion that kept us busy over the years and held us unaccountable to the real question.[80]

"The real question"—what is that? In most cases, I would say it's fairly straight forward with Jesus: *Do you believe in me?* How will blind men receive their sight? How will a lame man walk? How will thousands find food in the wilderness? How will Mary's broken heart be made whole again? Belief in Jesus. Jesus isn't just asking us about our belief in him with a direct question, as he did with Peter (Matt. 16:15). He's always asking, always looking for our confession. Jesus's whole purpose for coming here is summarized in what he calls "the work of God." What is this work? "That you believe in him whom [the Father] has sent" (John 6:29). *Belief in Jesus*—that's the deepest confession behind every little inquiry that emerges from us. And our confession of belief in every circumstance is that profession of deeper allegiance Whyte mentions, our greater dedication to the one beyond us. And it's also the more courageous road. In a thousand ways, we need to keep confessing the truth about who Jesus is.

Questions also help us *notice* where we are and how God's love meets us. God's question to Adam and Eve in Genesis 3:9 revealed just how far they had gone, not in distance but in depravity. Adam and Eve now thought they could hide from the ever-present God. Could they be any further from the truth? God's question was meant for them, not for him. His question drew their gaze to their fallen situation. But it also drew their gaze to grace and love. God didn't destroy them for rebelling. In fact, he would eventually give *himself* for them to make things right. And that is the most beautiful thing no human could imagine.

The same could be said of Jesus's questions to the blind man, to the lame man, to Philip, to Mary. Each question highlighted the need for God, the need for Christ, the need for redemption, for grace and love. These needs allow the hearers to notice where they are in relation to God and how God's love meets them. It's only when we've noticed where we are that we can see where we need to go. And we always need to go *with* God, into the beauty of communion.

The healing of a man possessed by demons led that man to beg for one thing: that he might be *with* Jesus (Luke 8:39). That's what we always want and need—to be with God. Remember what Vos said about our yearning for communion? Elsewhere he wrote,

> To be a Christian is to live one's life, not merely in obedience to God, nor merely in dependence on God, not even merely for the sake of God; it is to stand in conscious, reciprocal fellowship with God, to be identified with him in thought and purpose and work, to receive from him and give back to him in the ceaseless interplay of spiritual forces.[81]

To be in Christ is to realize with full hope that we always want to be with God. Jesus's questions helped people notice where they were and what they needed most: the presence of God, the most beautiful and kingly shepherd.

And here's the jewel in all this: that very thing—noticing our desire and need for God's presence—draws up that Christ-light inside us. Jesus knew that only this would satisfy us. Our covenantal, communion-seeking, always-reacting self needed the light of God. And Jesus's ministry is the message that while *they* needed to come to God, *God* had actually come to them. He revealed their need and offered the gift at the same time. This is the beauty of the gospel, the beauty of Christ. He shows us where we are while assuring us that he is here (Matt. 28:20).

APPLICATION

What about us? We can't ask questions as the omnipotent God. But we can still learn to ask questions that help other believers confess the truth and notice God's love and beauty. God in Christ asks us questions to draw out the light he put inside us and to bring us closer to himself. McHugh writes, "God asks questions to elicit dialogue, a true give-and-take, and he is genuinely, even astonishingly, interested in our responses."[82] And he waits for them. He knows we have things inside to work out. "In asking questions and holding back his answers, Jesus invites honesty, vulnerability, and intimacy."[83] Aren't you thankful that God comes to us with questions, drawing us into the beauty of relationship?

Do we use questions after this pattern? More often in our conversations, I think we're just waiting for our turn to speak. That's not real listening. And it certainly doesn't help fellow believers move toward confession and noticing. What can we do instead of waiting for our turn to speak?

Adam McHugh notes that asking the first question isn't the hard part. It's the second question, the follow-up, the response that shows we actually care about what's going on beneath the surface.[84] After asking someone an *open-ended* question (where a simple "yes" or "no" won't work), for instance, there will come a time where we can say, "Tell me more."[85] This is often unexpected, but "an unexpected question, asked at the right time, can open a whole world. The pace of the conversation at this point will often slow down, as the speaker realizes that you care about what she is saying and that you won't interject if she pauses to think or speak slowly."[86]

McHugh also notes that we can answer the questions of others with a question of our own. When some asks, "What's your favorite movie?" we might respond with, "Why do you ask?" Sometimes there isn't great depth behind another's question, but often there is. And your question can help someone process the emotions and motivations behind his question.

My father died of brain cancer when I was eighteen. My mother later remarried. After many years, a friend once asked me, "Was it hard for you when your mom started dating someone?" I knew there was more beneath the surface. I responded truthfully. "No—it didn't, though I'm not sure why. But . . . why do you ask?" That question set me up to listen. And there was much to listen to. Confession was forthcoming, as was noticing God's love and the beauty of his grace.

As we listen, we wait. We stay patient. And if the opportunity presents itself, we may have the chance to help a brother or sister move toward confession and noticing, to admitting what's troubling them and where they are in relation to God.

And we point them, of course, to the Christ-light they've already been given, to the one who hears our every confession as the great high priest and then shows us both where we are and where we need to be: *with* him.

There are artful ways to do this. And . . . not so artful ways. But rather than prescribing words for you, I would say that waiting until *after* the conversation ends to pose additional questions can be very comforting to others. There are two reasons for this.

First, it shows the person that you are *still* thinking of him or her—the hallmark of a great listener. Gifted listeners "keep hearing you" after the conversation has ended. They carry your words and concerns as precious cargo on the ship of their soul. And they return to your words frequently.

Second, this prevents us from dishing out answers like hotcakes. Giving ourselves time to think and pray about what we've heard goes a long way. I've found that the sort of response I want to give in the moment is very different from the sort I want to give later that day or the following one.

Questions are one of the greatest gifts language has to offer. They do far more than give us information. They can lead us to confession and noticing—turning our eyes back to the Christ-light burning inside us so we can glow brighter and closer to the Lord of light. Belief in him is always our ultimate confession. Communion with God is always where we belong.

Ask. Listen. Wait. And take your turn confessing and noticing.

REFLECT

1. What other effects do God's questions have in Scripture?

2. Request that a friend come up with a question to ask you. Write down your response, and then examine it for elements of *confession* and *noticing*.

3. Think of a question you could ask someone in your life. Ask it, and then wait for a full answer. Look for an opportunity to say, "Tell me more."

PRAY

God of questions,
God of answers,
Ask me something.
Help me confess:

Jesus, you are the Son of God.
Help me notice
My deep need for you.
And make me a patient listener,
Following questions with silence,
Inquiry with interest,
Revelation with encouragement.

SEEING LIGHT BY TELLING STORIES

JESUS USED QUESTIONS (AMONG other things) to help God's people notice their need for him and their longing for communion with the God of truth, love, and beauty. But he also used stories—parables. Why did he do this? Once again, what we think of stories hardly does them justice. Stories aren't just narratives that entertain; they're agents of change. Stories *define* and *direct* us, but they do so in a way that gives us ownership of the journey. Remember that carrying the Christ-light is a word journey, and we're always growing in our unique application of that light (contrast, variation, distribution).

JESUS'S PARABLES

Jesus's parables are famous, but his reliance on them as a teaching tool may be overlooked. Mark notes, "He did not speak to them without a parable, but privately to his own disciples he explained everything" (Mark 4:34). "Them" here refers to the common people. But why not explain things simply to the common people and save the symbolic stories for his disciples? Well, parables had a certain effect on people. Actually, they had several.

First, note that parables, as narratives, teach *indirectly*. Craig Blomberg writes, "Whenever we face a hostile audience, the indirect rhetoric of compelling stories may help at least some people hear God's word more favorably."[87] For example, I love to read books but am slower to apply what I've read until I write about the subject. You could come at me directly and say, "You need to slow down and read more thoughtfully so you can apply what God is teaching you." That would sting, and I would recoil.

Or you could you say,

> There once was a man with a great library—full of all the books you could imagine, shelf upon shelf, many books only reachable by a tall ladder. Each time he read a book, he would race back to the shelf, place it there carefully, and pull down another. But he was troubled because the more he read, the heavier he felt, and the harder it became to walk. One day, he decided not to read another book, but to page through the one he had just read. At the end of that day, he felt lighter. When he remarked on this to his servant, a wise old man, the servant replied, "Many books can weigh any soul down. We must wait for the words to grow wings."

If you said that, I might start to open the door of communication and confess my trouble. Why? Because I find *myself* in that story and receive instruction that seems to come from a sacred, hidden place. That leads to the next effect.

Second, parables invite us into the story, almost without our knowing. Blomberg notes, "The power of good fiction is that it grabs one's attention, sucks one into the plot, and makes one think it is about other people until it is too late."[88] In the story I just told, I would be identifying with the master of the library fairly early. And I would long to be the wise old servant by the end. The story would thus be teaching me without my knowing. I would think it's a story about others—until it's too late. This is how stories *define* and *direct* us. We find ourselves in the plot somehow (define) and emerge with a new perspective on where we should go (direct). We'll see this momentarily when we look at Mark 4:2–20.

Third, and related to the previous effect, parables reveal what we think of God. And in that sense, they distinguish and separate us from those who identify with a different character. In relation to the parable of the sower in Mark 4, Vern Poythress says, "Understanding a parable was not a matter that could be approached in a safe, antiseptic, neutral objectivity. The addressees were already committed. They found themselves already in process, already belonging to some kind of soil, already being questioned about the quality of their hearing. They were already for Jesus or against him (Matt. 12:30)."[89] We always carry with us assumptions about God, assumptions about Jesus. Jesus's parables brought those assumptions to the surface. As the light of the world, Jesus will always distinguish his followers from his opponents. And he often used parables to do just that.

Now, these three effects of parables help us see how stories *define* and *direct* us. They tell us who we are and where we're headed. (Note the similarity to the effects of questions, which help us *confess* and *notice*.) We've already discussed that who we are is bound up with our complex imitation of God as unique, covenantal, communion-seeking, ever-reacting-to-revelation creatures. Our direction comes in one of those areas, or in one of the areas of the *lex Christi*, or in an area identified elsewhere in our reading of Scripture. But let's look for the moment at the three areas of *covenant, communion*, and *revelation*.

- How do I stand in covenantal relation to God right now? Am I living in Christ by the Spirit or living in Adam by rebellion? What aspects of my "old self" need to be cast off in the Spirit?

- How am I communing with God today? How am I drawing near to him? What stands between us?

- In what ways am I reacting to God's revelation all around me? Where and how is my heart lacking gratitude and praise?

Let's look at this in the context of Mark 4:2–20.

> And he was teaching them many things in parables, and in his teaching he said to them: "Listen! Behold, a sower went out to sow. And as he sowed, some seed fell along the path, and the birds came and devoured it. Other seed fell on rocky ground, where it did not have much soil, and immediately it sprang up, since it had no depth of soil. And when the sun rose, it was scorched, and since it had no root, it withered away. Other seed fell among thorns, and the thorns grew up and choked it, and it yielded no grain. And other seeds fell into good soil and produced grain, growing up and increasing and yielding thirtyfold and sixtyfold and a hundredfold." And he said, "He who has ears to hear, let him hear." And when he was alone, those around him with the twelve asked him about the parables. And he said to them, "To you has been given the secret of the kingdom of God, but for those outside everything is in parables, so that
>
> "'they may indeed see but not perceive, and may indeed hear but not understand, lest they should turn and be forgiven.'" And he said to them, "Do you not understand this parable? How then will you understand all the parables? The sower sows the word. And these are the ones along the path, where the word is sown: when they hear, Satan immediately comes and takes away the word that is sown in them. And these are the ones sown on rocky ground: the ones who, when they hear the word, immediately receive it with joy. And they have no root in themselves, but endure for a while; then, when tribulation or persecution arises on account of the word, immediately they fall away. And others are the ones sown among thorns. They are

those who hear the word, but the cares of the world and the deceitfulness of riches and the desires for other things enter in and choke the word, and it proves unfruitful. But those that were sown on the good soil are the ones who hear the word and accept it and bear fruit, thirtyfold and sixtyfold and a hundredfold."

Ask yourself a series of questions that will help *define* and *direct* you.

- What substance does Jesus use to represent us in this parable? What does this imagery suggest about who we are?

- Which type of soil do you most readily identify with? Why?

- Which of the threats to good growth is most harmful to you? What can you pray about and seek God's help for in the midst of that threat?

I'll illustrate with myself before suggesting how all this relates to the Christ-light and how we might incorporate this in our own relationships.

First, Jesus represents us as soil in this parable. Soil is filled with nutrients—life-giving grace that God gives. We are rich because of divine bestowal. We can learn and love and create and speak because of *him*. But because our souls are nutrient rich, we're always growing something. Always. At least, something is always attempting to take root in us, even if our rocky callousness shoulders it away. We're never empty, never neutral. We're always worshiping, in other words. As Poythress wrote, "The alternative to worshiping God is not worshiping nothing, but worshiping a substitute, worshiping a counterfeit. And the counterfeit must be sufficiently successful to give the illusion of satisfying our needs and longing for God."⁹⁰ In the parable from Mark 4, the counterfeits are the thorns. Thorns have roots, of course. They penetrate our souls and reveal that something is growing, something that gives us temporary hope and fulfillment. But above the soil are only things to draw our blood, not to deepen our communion with God, which is our core passion as image-bearers.

Second, I most readily identify with this thorny soil. I grew up poor—not in a way that put us on the street, but my father was a pastor of a small church, and getting a brain tumor diagnosis at 37 meant a host of medical bills. My mother developed an astonishing number of colon polyps at the same time, which can quickly lead to cancer if not removed. So, we were hit on both parental fronts with major health issues. My father did carpentry on the side and preached on the weekends—a bit like Jesus did, I guess. All things considered, though we had enough to get by and God always provided, money was more than tight, which led to me being enamored with people who had it.

That's where the thorns started to grow. I was so far removed from money that those who possessed it seemed to hold some secret to life. And I still struggle to disbelieve that lie. Materialism and earthly wealth are continual threats to my steadfastness in faith. I have to remind myself of Jesus's words to the rich young ruler. Wealth wasn't the key to gaining more from life; it was the key that locked him away from life in God. He went away sad, leaving the presence of the light of the world, because the thorns and thistles of wealth took up all his soil space. Letting go of wealth seemed like letting go of everything. But that's just how heart soil works: whatever takes root inside you starts to crowd out lesser loves.

That's why I see those thorns as the most threatening to the good seed of the gospel. It's easy for a garden to be overtaken by weeds. All we have to do is *nothing*. Without constant tending, our garden soil *will* grow competitors to the greenery of God. We must tend to the soil by the Spirit, immersing our hearts in the words of God as the Christ-light grows in us.

Do you see how Jesus's parable *defines* and *directs* me? Who

I am—a God-imitating, covenant-bound, communion-seeking, ever-reacting soul—is constantly under threat. The allure of wealth pushes me away from faithfulness (covenant), away from communion, away from seeing and hearing God (reaction). That's because Satan's chief purpose is to dim the very light Christ ignited in me. I need reminders of who I really am in Christ, of what fulfills my deepest needs and longings. And I need reminders about where I'm going. Because of the Spirit's work in me, I can always sense when my heart wants to turn its shoulders toward material success. Jesus redirects me with the story of his self-giving. He *owned* everything only to *give* everything, and then to gain the sheep he sought. The parable of the sower reveals my assumptions about God and what is truly *good* in the world.

APPLICATION

Jesus's parables affected his listeners by teaching them indirectly, inviting them into a story, and using that story to reveal what they thought about God. He let his listeners make their own journey toward identification and redirection, pointing to himself as the light they longed for. Just as with his questions, the parables he told were for us, not for him. They work on us today by prying open our stubborn, ever-wandering hearts.

But this isn't a call to start telling parables to your neighbor. We wouldn't be able to do what Jesus did as the parable expert, nor should we try. People need to be identified and redirected toward Christ, not toward us.

Still, there is something to be said for telling stories to others, not just fictional ones but the flesh and blood stories of our own lives. I firmly believe God *wants* us to tell stories to each other because, like the parables of Jesus, stories define and direct us. And they do so in a way far less confrontational than formal advice would. People will find themselves in our stories. And, God willing, by the time they realize it, it will be too late. They will notice something about who they are and where they're headed.

What are your stories? Write one down or tell it to a friend and see just how much it helps someone else experience definition and direction in their own context.

I'll end by sharing one of these stories of mine, and then we'll take a look at one last method Jesus used to open people to his light: forgiveness.

> Recently, I took a pair of gray suede boots into another room in our house to brush them clean. I'd just worn them to a farm and tramped through the soft dirt path of a corn maze with my son. I rubbed at the tips of each boot with an eraser, taking most of the mud and staining off. Then I used a soft bristle brush to remove the suede dust and flecks of dirt. I looked with approval at the cleaned boots, and as I went to set them down, my son, who had run through the golden corn with me an hour earlier, said, "Dad, what are you doing?" I hadn't noticed him watching. "Just cleaning the stains off my boots." He looked perplexed and then said with confidence, "But if you always clean off your shoes, how will you remember all the adventures you've had?"

How does that story help you understand who you are? How does it help direct you?

Reflect

1. In what sense do stories help you remember who you are? In what ways do they direct you?

2. What's a story Jesus told that defines and directs you?

3. What's a story someone else once told you that defined and directed you toward God?

PRAY

My story-telling Lord,
You don't just tell stories;
You wield them like wind.
The doors of my heart
Are thrown to the wall,
And you whistle into my deepest places.
Your stories tell me who I am.
Your stories teach me where to go.
Keep speaking.
Open me to your stories.
And show me the stories of my own life,
Stories *you* have woven together
In a raw and beautiful tapestry.
Help me tell them.
Help me listen.

Unrestricted Forgiveness

Everyone knows about Jesus's famous teaching that we should forgive others without end—seventy times seven (Matt. 18:22). But Jesus's entire life, from another perspective, was a giant act of forgiveness. And this led him to fill our lives with his light.

In Ephesians 5, Paul is addressing those whom Christ has saved. We examined this passage at the outset, but look at it once more. "At one time you were darkness, but now you are light in the Lord. Walk as children of light (for the fruit of light is found in all that is good and right and true)" (Eph. 5:8–9).

God didn't just brighten us, as if something inside us were already giving off light. Remember, we were doused wicks, letting off our noxious fumes into the good creation of God. We didn't need improvement; we needed salvation, a new identity. And so Christ made us *children of light*. Light is our family now. The Father of lights is *our* Father. How? How could created wicks of callous sinners blaze for eternity with God—after not only running from the light but assaulting it? Within the larger mysterious reason of God's love is a smaller reason, something we needed if we were to be candles lit with Christ: *forgiveness*.

Christ's Life as Forgiveness

Forgiveness is a deeply mysterious gift. It's an act of dam-breaking. Let me explain.

In relationships, water is flowing and carrying both people forward. Love and intimacy require two people to drift together on the currents of experience. They witness the same passing shoreline, each from his own perspective. Their differences harmonize in their joint presence and communication.

But when things go wrong, when one is hurt by the other, separation sets in between them. And that is an evil we too quickly dismiss. We treat isolation as somewhat neutral these days, and independence as a virtue. But the Christian linguist I studied for years once wrote, "Isolation is the road to hell."[91] In my illustration, it's the *river* to hell. With matching clarity, he noted that "if a person succeeds in becoming independent, he dies."[92] We not only need our environment to live; we need *people*. That's part of what it means to be a covenant-bound, communion-seeking creature. Isolation and independence are antithetical to our true humanity. We are made to be *with* God and *with* others. We are *with*-creatures.

But when one person is wronged in a relationship, which is bound to happen daily in a broken world, separation sets in, and a dam is raised, cutting off one person from the other. Forgiveness is the spiritual gift of dam-breaking, opening the channel once more between persons, bringing relational unity where isolation and independence reigned. But this dam-breaking is costly. It's never free.

Now, apply this on a cosmic scale to the coming of Christ. We have not merely one relationship between the Trinity and a human, but billions upon billions—relationships more numerous than stardust spread across a thousand galaxies. So. Many. Relationships. So many rivulets between God and people, so many life-giving waterways. But sin meant that every one of them had a dam. Every single one, since all have sinned against God and need forgiveness (Rom. 3:23).

Christ's coming broke ten billion dams. The mere entrance of Christ into the world of humanity was a colossal act of dam-breaking.

But the cost was more than we can fathom. In his book *Forgive*, Tim Keller writes, "To forgive someone's debt to you is to absorb the debt yourself.... Forgiveness means the cost of the wrong moves from the perpetrator to you, and you bear it."[93] He continues, "Forgiveness, then, is a form of voluntary suffering. In forgiving, rather than retaliating, you make a choice to bear the cost."[94] God *voluntarily* bore the cost of billions upon billions, tiny, vein-like relational rivers all clogged and muddied by the debris of selfishness.

In opening each waterway, Jesus makes his way to us, and then he allows us to gaze at the light of *God*. It's this loving, relational, voluntarily-suffering, dam-breaking God that we image. By his whole life, as a grand act of divine forgiveness, Jesus draws back the curtain of our rebellion so we can stare at *this* God, at the Father of lights (James 1:17), who lit a candle in our chest through Christ, a candle that would help us seek out our family members.

I was reminded of this when I read Dallas Willard discussing Proverbs 20:27. The KJV translation puts it in a way that resonates with the theme of this book. "The spirit of man is the candle of the LORD, searching all the inward parts of the belly." Yes—the candle of the Lord. "The spirit of the individual truly is ... the 'candle of the Lord,' in the light of which we see ourselves and our world as God sees."[95] Willard links this candle to our self-awareness as new creatures in Christ.

> The soul's self-awareness applies to every part of the self: it touches upon one's family, possessions, profession and health; it reaches to one's fear of death, attitudes toward God, sexuality, preoccupation with reputation, concern with appearance and countless other areas of one's life. Our spirit, as a candle in the Lord's hands, may shed light on many other things apart from our own internal condition, although the primary point of the passage from Proverbs is the illumination of the inner life.[96]

The candle of the Lord could only ever be lit in us through Christ, for apart from him we *are* darkness (Eph. 5:8). Because of sin, we *need* forgiveness. Otherwise, we cannot be lit with the light of God and dwell with the Father of lights. And that forgiveness, to switch metaphors, broke the sinful dam we'd built between us and God. It let the water flow again, under the light of Christ.

> The rivers ran, sweet, clear, and cold
> As we swam near the God of light,
> Bound by a brightness, pure and bold,
> That kept us from eternal night.
> But we went off to chase a dream
> Of being gods ourselves, alone.
> We built a dam to hold the stream,
> To stay the Lord of flesh and bone.
> But God would not sit idly by.
> With one colossal surge of love
> He sent himself, alone to die,
> Broke dams below with power above.
> All waterways are open, friend.
> The dams are cleared; the water's right.
> We commune and stare, beyond our end,
> As infant candles toward the light.

Our Forgiving and God's Forgiving

While our forgiveness is not the same as God's—since he forgives as the all-powerful Creator and we forgive as dependent creatures—our forgiveness is based on God's. It's yet another way in which we can imitate him. Our seeing the Christ-light in our brothers and sisters can only happen when we've seen our own desperate need for forgiveness met in him.

Why is this the case? Because true forgiveness flows from a changed *heart*, not a resolution simply to "do the right thing." As Tim Keller put it, "divine mercy should change our *hearts* so that we are able to forgive as God forgave us. If we will not offer others forgiveness, it shows that we did not truly repent and receive God's."[97]

This shouldn't surprise us. God is the origin of all good. His gifts grant life and redemption. God creates by *giving*; he re-creates by *for*giving. If we want to share in the work of God, we must be well-practiced in the voluntary suffering that is forgiveness.

But how?

FORGIVENESS AS A PERSPECTIVE SHIFT

Keller suggests that true, deep forgiveness, what he calls *heart forgiveness*, "includes *identifying with the wrongdoer, inwardly paying the debt*, and then *willing good for the wrongdoer*."[98] Doing this involves a perspective shift, which we commonly refer to with the word *empathy*. To identify with someone is to see the world from his perspective. We often treat this as absurd in the context of forgiveness. But the Apostle Paul suggests it isn't absurd; it's required.

Paul says he is the "worst" or "foremost" of sinners (1 Tim. 1:15). Yet, not only had Paul just told us a few verses earlier that he was judged "faithful by Christ" (v. 12), but he's arguably the most influential missionary of all time, and he wrote much of the New Testament. He also risked his life multiple times for the sake of the gospel. If Paul is the "worst," what's that say about *us*?

Paul isn't making an objective statement here that puts him at the bottom rung of Christianity. He's expressing an honest perspective—his self-perspective. How does Paul see *himself*? As the worst of sinners, in most need of God's grace. In other words, Paul doesn't start his self-assessment by comparing himself to others. He stares at his spiritual state. He's a fallen image-bearer in need of grace through Christ Jesus. Apart from Christ, Paul really is the "worst" and the darkest. So am I. And so are you.

This is very hard for us to accept because we're so used to measuring moral value horizontally. We assess goodness and righteousness based on how different we think we are from our neighbor. But that's the wrong standard—and a low bar. Paul looks vertically. He stares at the glory of the risen Christ who blinded him on the Damascus road, and says, "Yea, in relation to *him*, I'm the worst of sinners. I'm at the bottom." To suggest that *anyone* is beneath us is to claim some level of righteousness on our own. And for fallen humanity, "self-generated righteous people" is an empty set. As Paul himself said to the Romans, following Psalms 14 and 53, "There is no one righteous; not even one; there is no one who understands; there is no one who seeks God" (Rom. 3:10–11). John Murray didn't mince words. "With reference to God all men are noetically blind and in respect of Godward aspiration they are dead."[99] Blind and dead. Apart from Christ, that's Paul. That's you. That's me. We're all the worst since, as Cornelius Van Til wrote, "there are no degrees in the principle of depravity."[100] There is no one in *lesser* need of Christ than another. That's beautiful, when you think about it. But it's tough to accept. And that's because we're bent in on ourselves.

I often ruminate on the Latin phrase used by Saint Augustine and later by John Calvin: *incurvatus in se*. We are "curved in on ourselves." We see ourselves as primary, all-important, and better than a host of others. We think, "I need the gospel, but Hitler *really* needed it." We stare at the Hitlers of history and say, "I'm nothing like *that*." Actually, you are. And so am I. Why? Because there are no gradations to depravity. We are all equally in need of Christ. And yet we have a major problem seeing the sins of others in ourselves.[101] This is perhaps the greatest barrier to forgiveness.

Fyodor Dostoevsky addressed this powerfully in *The Brothers Karamazov*. The wise priest, Father Zosima, seemed to echo Paul's sentiment when he said,

> There can be no judge of a criminal on earth until the judge knows that he, too, is a criminal, exactly the same as the one who stands before him, and that he is perhaps most guilty of all for the crime of

the one standing before him. When he understands this, then he will be able to be a judge. However mad that may seem, it is true. For if I myself were righteous, perhaps there would be no criminal standing before me now.[102]

Zosima had similar words to the young Alyosha before he entered the monastery. "When he knows that he is not only worse than all those in the world, but is also guilty before all people, on behalf of all and for all, for all human sins, the world's and each person's, only then will the goal of our unity be achieved."[103]

That sounds insane to our Western individualist ears, doesn't it? But Father Zosima was merely following the Apostle Paul in seeing himself as the worst of all sinners. All Zosima draws out is the perspective shift. We must open our eyes and not see just ourselves (*incurvatus in se*) but *ourselves in others*. The atrocities of others are faint echoes of the atrocities in *us*. When we fail to see ourselves in others, we cannot forgive. And when we cannot forgive, we cannot see the Christ-light burning in our brothers and sisters. And if we cannot see the Christ-light in them, why are we so convinced that it's in us?

Thomas Merton wrote strikingly,

> The devil makes many disciples by preaching against sin. He convinces them of the great evil of sin, induces a crisis of guilt by which "God is satisfied," and after that he lets them spend the rest of their lives meditating on the intense sinfulness and evident reprobation of other men.[104]

Rich Villodas remarks, "by becoming solely focused on abstaining from sin (defined very narrowly), we live by a crushing moralism that robs us from enjoying God and self-righteously places us above others."[105] When we place ourselves above others, that makes it impossible for us to see ourselves in them. We can't look people in the eyes when we're standing above them.

If we want to see ourselves in others, we have to start where Paul did. We have to let go of the falsehood that we are better than them. We have to see ourselves as the worst, as having no one beneath us, and then we'll always be able to see something of ourselves in the wrongs committed against us. That alone can bring empathy.

But what follows empathy is our refocusing on the Christ-light, the hope of glory God has lit inside another human soul. Knowing that Christ indwells our brother or sister, we can ask a string of questions. The following ones are related to covenant, communion, and revelation, but we could ask additional questions about any sense in which we image God.

- **How might this person be relating to God right now in covenant?** Is there frustration? Doubt? Fear? Pride? Distraction? Is there assurance of salvation in Christ?

- **In what ways do this person's actions reflect a longing for communion?** What might be substituting for that communion? What substitutes are reflected in our own spiritual battles?

- **In what ways is this person reacting to God's revelation all around us?** Is there gratitude? Worship? Wonder? Is there ignorance and envy? Can we identify forms of the same vices in ourselves?

Asking questions is a start to seeing someone else's story, to seeing the world through his eyes, and that leads to empathy, which cuts a path to forgiveness. Once we can empathize with another follower of Christ, we can forgive out of a sense of gratitude for Christ forgiving us of similar sins.

But I want to end this chapter by reminding us where all this fits in the theme for this book. Jesus is the light inside his people.

He not only gives it, but maintains it by the Spirit, constantly drawing it forward and diminishing the remaining darkness. As his followers, we're called to take up the same light-seeking work. Forgiveness is critical in all this because just as light and love go together (for God is light and love), darkness and sin go together. That's why the Old and New Testaments associate moral failings with darkness. Even Paul does this in Romans 1:21 when he describes sinful hearts as "darkened." Sin is heart-darkness—a darkness that hugs the Christ-light in our chest, making it hard for others to see what God has done and is doing in us. Where and how does God dispel this darkness? Through the light of his self-giving *love*, and forgiveness is the very thing that breaks down the door of darkness. Forgiveness recognizes that "at its core, sin is failure to love."[106] Failure to love—both God and neighbor—brings darkness, shrouding the covenant-keeping, communion-seeking, ever-reacting light inside us.

Forgiveness dispels the darkness. It calls each guilty party back into the light, the light of love. It's no coincidence that followers of Christ are to be known *by* their love (John 13:35) and known *as* children of light (Eph. 5:8). Love and light are bound together—as two great trees with interwoven root systems. The path between them in a broken world is forgiveness. Seeing the light in others is a constant call to forgive, to bear the suffering of others and use the very power of God's Spirit to call them back into the brightness of God, whose forgiveness of sin in Christ is what lit their candle at the start.

We've now talked about seeing as a servant, seeing the sheep, using questions, teaching through stories, and forgiving others. These are the Christ-given resources we have for seeing his light in God's people. But it would help to summarize what the brightening of our light looks like as the Spirit works in us. How do we identify the Christ-light and encourage it in others? We've dealt with this indirectly throughout the book, but the next chapter will bring several points together to focus our attention. In the final chapter, we'll look at the motive behind our use of all these resources: *love*.

Reflect

1. What keeps you from forgiving someone else?

2. What has been the effect on your soul when someone forgives you?

3. What are the greatest barriers you face when trying to empathize with others?

Pray

God, to create us, you gave.
To re-create us, you *for*gave.
You broke ten billion dams
So we could come to you.
But it was *you* who came to us.
The darkness of sin
Was blocking our light.
You wiped away the black,
And gave our lives back.
And now you call us ever higher,
As children of the light.
Help us to see what you did for us,
And then to turn and see our old selves
In the wrongs of others.
And as we see ourselves in them,
May we forgive,
And make light.

WHAT BRIGHTENING LOOKS LIKE

The Christ-light is the indwelling resurrection life of our Lord and savior, making us alive to the Spirit, filling us with hope, and anchoring our souls in the will, heart, and work of God. But this can all seem very abstract. And if we don't know what this Christ-light looks like more specifically, the call to see that light in other believers, and even to work with the Spirit to apply it to our own lives, will take a back seat. All I aim to do here is draw out specifics based on the areas of covenant, communion, and reaction.

Covenant

A covenant, we noted earlier, is a relationship with guidelines—set up with curses for disobedience and blessings for faithfulness. God is the one who approached us to make this covenant. And because God is holy, if we want to be in relationship with him, *we* must be holy. We must match him on the creaturely level, imitating his holiness as we imitate anything else we're able to as creatures. The thing at stake in a covenant is *faithfulness*. The same is true for imitation. How well does the imitation represent and glorify the original?

Faithfulness and imitation was present from the very beginning with Adam. Adam and Eve *knew* they were in covenant with God, and that knowledge was the basis for their faithfulness. Vos writes,

> Since Adam was perfect in every respect, along with his natural relationship to God belonged a completely clear awareness of this relationship. He knew from nature, by innate knowledge, what God could demand of him—that he stood, as bearer of the image of God, under the moral opposition between good and evil, that upon breaking this natural relationship punishment would follow. All this and still more: He was assured of the favor of God and of life, provided that he persevered in the good. All this Adam could know naturally. Fallen man still knows the same by nature.[107]

The thing at stake for Adam and Eve, and for us, is *faithfulness*, being true to the terms of the covenant—not because the covenant is some legal code set up by a micromanaging God, but because the covenant is an act of *love* and a path to lasting *freedom* in relationship with God. We have a warped sense of freedom, assuming that true freedom is complete independence, void of restrictions. But we are always free *to* something or someone. We're always in relationship, always in service to someone or something, even if that someone is ourselves. Covenant is pervasive. That's why John Frame can say, "everything and everybody is in covenant with God."[108] And if everything and everyone is in *relationship* with God, then it would make sense for *faithfulness* to be a governing principle of existence.

The question we can ask ourselves and others when thinking about the Spirit of Christ working to brighten the Christ-light inside us is simple: *Are you faithful?* This question, with all its offshoots and applications, reveals where we are in our covenant, our relationship, with God. Someone growing in faithfulness to God and his word in a particular facet—in prayer, for example—is thus "brightening."

Jesus Christ called those whom he healed and taught them to lead a faithful life, to leave a life of sin and to declare the good works of God (Matt. 5:16, 19–20; John 5:14; 8:11). Jesus offered himself to others by faith and then called them to faithfulness. That faithfulness is detailed in specific actions throughout the New Testament. In Philippians 4:8, Paul says, "whatever is true, whatever is honorable, whatever is just, whatever is pure, whatever is lovely, whatever is commendable, if there is any excellence, if there is anything worthy of praise, think about these things." He gets even more specific in passages such as 1 Peter 2:1, telling the people to "put away all malice and all deceit and hypocrisy and envy and all slander." You could also generate a sort of opposites list based on Romans 1:29–32.

> They were filled with all manner of unrighteousness, evil, covetousness, malice. They are full of envy, murder, strife, deceit, maliciousness. They are gossips, slanderers, haters of God, insolent, haughty, boastful, inventors of evil, disobedient to parents, foolish, faithless, heartless, ruthless. Though they know God's righteous decree that those who practice such things deserve to die, they not only do them but give approval to those who practice them.

Taking the opposites of this hideous list would produce something like this list of character traits. A brightening Christian soul . . .

- longs for righteousness

- shows loving kindness

- gives generously

- shows good will

- practices selflessness

- protects the weak
- tells the truth
- loves silence and assumes the best of others (instead of gossiping)
- speaks graciously of others (rather than slandering)
- respects parents and figures of authority
- is meek
- obeys when disobedience would be easier
- seeks wisdom (submitting to God's word)
- empathizes with others
- shows mercy
- gives grace

That's what brightening can look like in the context of God's Christ-fulfilled covenant. It may be a helpful practice to choose *one* of these areas for a week and ask the Spirit to give you opportunities to grow.

Communion

When it comes to communion, it's a matter of wanting to be in the presence of God, longing to speak with him and waiting for him to speak back in the Spirit as you read his word. What's at stake in communion is *love*, namely choosing God above all lesser loves.

The question we can ask ourselves and others when thinking about the brightening work of Christ is this: *Do you love God?* This question is linked with the previous one, since Jesus said that those who love him will do the works of God (John 14:15). But it's much more than that. There's a difference between *doing* and *being*.

I'm not trying to be philosophical; just think of it in the context of a relationship. I've talked with older people who sometimes have friendships or a marriage in which silence plays a prominent role. Rather than only seeking to *do* things with those they love (traveling, dining out, exercising), they simply want to *be with* the other. The presence is the passion. This is especially true and beautiful for couples who have been married for decades. There is less of a focus on *doing* things and more emphasis on *being* together. Both are important, of course. You can link hands with a spouse and walk side by side, doing marvelous things for God's kingdom, and seeing beautiful things in the world. But you can also sit in a hospital waiting room with your spouse and not utter a word, both of you knowing that your presence is sufficient.

Do you like just *being with God*? Do you ever just sit in a room with him, or pray openly on a cross-country run, or smile at him when you see the gold-bellied geese cackle and wave across a Pennsylvania sunset in November?

And when you talk about God, is something stirred inside you, as if you're talking about a love deeper than time itself? Would someone listen to you and say, "Wow, he *loves* being with the Lord"?

Put differently, is God *enough* for you? Or are you always chasing something else? Brightening as a communion-seeking creature comes with a passionate, soul-deep plea just to be in the same room with him. And a wide smile when you realize he's already there.

This is one of the reasons I love reading Annie Dillard. She reminds me of my wild passion for a wild God, an untameable artist, and my spot in all the turning and twisting of his living canvas. Watch her reflect and ruminate on the rising and falling motion of life.

> It all happens so dizzyingly fast. The goldfinch I had seen was asleep in a thicket; when she settled to sleep, the weight of her breast locked her toes around her perch. Wasps were asleep with their legs hanging loose, their jaws jammed into the soft stems of plants. Everybody grab a handle: we're spinning headlong down. I am puffed clay, blown up and set down. That I fall like Adam is not surprising: I plunge, waft, arc, pour, and dive. The surprise is how good the wind feels on my face as I fall. And the other surprise is that I ever rise at all. I rise when I receive, like grass. I didn't know, I never have known, what spirit it is that descends into my lungs and flaps near my heart like an eagle rising. I named it full-of-wonder, highest good, voices. I shut my eyes and saw a tree stump hurled by wind, an enormous tree stump sailing sideways across my vision, with a wide circular brim of roots and soil like a tossed top hat. And what if those grasshoppers had been locusts descending, I thought, and what if I stood awake in a swarm? I cannot ask for more than to be so wholly acted upon, flown at, and lighted on in throngs, probed, knocked, even bitten. A little blood from the wrists and throat is the price I would willingly pay for that pressure of clacking weights on my shoulders, for the scent of deserts, groundfire in my ears—for being so in the clustering thick of things, rapt and enwrapped in the rising and falling real world.[109]

Of course, I'd say she *does* know that Spirit that descends into her lungs and flaps near her heart, and mine. It's my God. It's the wild one. It's the worker of wind and woodgrains, the shaper of sunsets and sunrises, the Light-smyth, the guardian of grasshopper and goldfinch. God takes my breath away (even though he gave it to me in the first place). I want more of *him*, and less of every lesser love.

That's what brightening looks like in the context of communion. In what ways can you position yourself to enjoy the pure presence of God? What activities make you feel closer to him? What spots of the day can you set aside for silent listening, just enjoying the company of the God who beats inside and around you?

REACTING TO REVELATION

Lastly, we have revelation, and our constant reaction to it. In God's general revelation, he reveals his attributes. In his special revelation (Scripture), he reveals the path to redemption, the path of himself in the person of Christ. But in both cases, the thing at stake is *reception*.

We're bombarded with so much each day in the physical world. Dallas Willard talks about this bombardment as a daily "bludgeoning."

> The visible world daily bludgeons us with its things and events. They pinch and pull and hammer away at our bodies. Few people arise in the morning as hungry for God as they are for cornflakes or toast and eggs. But instead of shouting and shoving, the *spiritual* world whispers at us every so gently. And it appears both at the edges and in the middle of events and things in the so-called real world of the visible.[110]

Amidst this bludgeoning, our hearts and minds grow layer after layer of dead skin around them. It seems like the only way to protect ourselves from the onslaught. But in protecting ourselves from the onslaught of information, we grow less practiced at reacting to revelation, at sensing and responding to the *spiritual* world—though even *not* reacting much to revelation is a sort of reaction.

We can have all sorts of reactions to God's revelation in nature and in Scripture, so this category is a bit unwieldy. Here are some common responses to God's revelation in nature.

- Awe
- Worship
- Fear (reverence)
- Joy
- Fixation
- Mourning (natural disasters)
- Excitement
- Deeper faith

Responses to God's revelation in Scripture might include the following (note some of the overlap).

- Repentance
- Gratitude
- Mercy
- Grace
- Forgiveness
- Worship
- Joy
- Freedom of mind (absence of anxiety)

- Compassion

- Deeper love for God

- Hope

- Courage

- Selflessness

- Humility

- Kindness

You could make your own list. These are just some of the reactions we have. I've mostly listed the positive ones, but remember that there are plenty of negative reactions in both categories, too: ignorance, anger, envy, selfishness, anxiety, grief, apathy, destructive behavior. The point is that we're *always* reacting. The real question is whether we're opening ourselves to *receiving* what God is saying about himself. Reception is always the thing at stake for revelation.

The question we can ask ourselves and others when thinking about the brightening work of Christ here is this: *Do you hear God?* I'm not talking about an audible voice inside your head. I'm talking about the speech of God in nature and in Scripture. God's revelation is a kind of speech. Are we hearing it, and how are we receiving and responding to it?

One truth I've found helpful is to recognize that God's "voice" follows us around as we hide his words in our hearts and minds, since we now have "the mind of Christ" (1 Cor. 2:16). Paul elsewhere says that God is renewing our minds, that the Spirit is ever working out a "metamorphosis in the seat of consciousness," a complete change in *how* and *what* we think.[111] The thoughts you have can thus be instances of receiving and embracing God's speech to you in Scripture (for Scripture *is* God's speech to us).

This can feel strange to us because we have a rigid understanding of a passage such as Isaiah 55:8, where God says plainly, "my thoughts are not your thoughts, neither are your ways my ways." That verse, however, comes right *after* a call to repentance. Once we have repented and accepted Christ as savior, God opens his mind to us as his creatures; he shares his thoughts with us on a creaturely level. How else could we have the mind of Christ? This doesn't mean we know things as the Almighty does, that our thoughts are divine. But it certainly means the thoughts that enter a Christian's mind can and very well should be colored by the thoughts of God from Scripture. It takes much work and prayerful reliance on the Spirit for that to happen, but it *will* happen. Again, this makes perfect sense if in accepting the Christ-light, we become homes for God's will (Father), heart (Son), and work (Spirit).

And so "the thoughts and feelings in the mind and spirit of one who is surrendered to God should be treated as if God were walking through one's personality with a candle, directing one's attention to things one after another."[112] Isn't that a beautiful image? Once more, this doesn't mean our minds won't battle lies. They certainly will![113] But that should *never* lead us to assume that all of our thoughts are corrupted lies. If we have the mind of Christ, we should be on the lookout for the thoughts of Christ—thoughts set on the pages of Scripture. And one theme of those thoughts will be our perceptions of and responses to the world around us, God's revelation.

Summary

The point of this chapter was to outline what "brightening" looks like as Christ works in us and in his people around us. We should have enough comfort with this content to answer those three basic questions about ourselves each day. Imagine God asking them. These are questions he's asking everyone in Christ. Each one is a country all its own.

- Are you faithful?

- Do you love me?

- Do you hear me?

Brightening happens deep in the woods of these countries. In the last chapter, we explore the motive for our brightening in Christ: *love*.

REFLECT

1. Which area (covenant, communion, reaction) presents the most challenges for you? How do you respond to those challenges?

2. What are some ways you could make time to enjoy God's presence more each day?

3. How do you find yourself responding to God's revelation? Choose something from nature, and then something from Scripture. Take some time to see how your heart is responding to what you see and read. How are the thoughts you have reflective of God's thoughts as revealed in Scripture?

PRAY

Jesus, my Light-smyth,
You expand my glow in the Spirit.
Help me to be faithful in the small things,
To draw closer to you in love.
Help me to enjoy simply being in your presence.
And show me how I'm reacting to you.
I want to be brighter in you,
So help me to abide in you
In will, heart, and work.

LOVE AND GIVING

Now we come to it: the final chapter. The point of this chapter is to focus on the motive for our brightening in Christ. A secondary point is to suggest what it means to *love* God and others, especially as we strive to see the Christ-light in God's people and in ourselves.

As we've seen over and over again, what Christ did in putting his light in us is ultimately an act of *love*. But what does love look like in daily life? We get plenty of examples from Jesus—the love of God with eyes and ears and fingers and a face.

Let me set out the principle I see in the gospels and end with some examples. These examples should help you love the light you see in God's people. It will take constant work and many failures, but remember this: "it is God who works in you, both to will and to work for his good pleasure" (Phil. 2:13). The Spirit is working in us. The Father's will is ours. The Son's heart is ours. We don't love the light in others on our own. The very God who lit the candle in your chest and mine is at the helm of our heart-ship. Take courage and confidence in that! This isn't an exercise in "trying harder." It's an exercise in listening to God and letting him lead you with the love of Christ that already indwells you.

The Principle of Christ

What does love look like, as that sacred act of approaching the light in other believers and working to brighten it? It looks like *going low and giving much*. It's a divine blend of humility and self-giving. Humility is putting others first; self-giving is the currency we use to pay for it.

As with all things good and true, the model comes from God himself—Father, Son, and Holy Spirit. These three are *one*—more intimate than we can fathom. In *Love Walked among Us*, Paul E. Miller writes, "Love is a journey into joy, a movement toward another person that results in intimacy, in oneness."[114] In reflecting on Jesus's words to his Father in John 17:10, Miller paraphrases, "I own nothing—I give it all to you. You own nothing—you give it all to me. Neither of us holds anything back. Our trust in each other is total."[115] That's how the Father loves the Son in the power of the Spirit. That's how the Son loves the Father in the power of the Spirit. They are "in" each other (17:21). They are one. This beautiful oneness applies on a creaturely level to us.

> Oneness is a state of pure and constant compassion devoid of selfishness. Your needs are so totally mine that "I am in you." My needs are so totally yours that "you are in me." We have no secrets—our hearts touch each other's fully. Each of us gives to the other all we have. Our joy is complete in each other.[116]

Jesus opens this flower of oneness, of love, before others. He humbles himself, "by taking the form of a servant" (Phil. 2:7), and then he gives himself to others. That's how he enters a feast with tax collectors and sinners (Matt. 9:10–13; Mark 2:13–22; Luke 5:27–37). That's how he touches a leper (Matt. 8:3; Mark 1:40–44; Luke 5:12–14). That's how he makes his own mud to heal a blind man (John 9:6). He humbles himself so that he sits *below* those whom he wants to love. And then he gives something of himself—his time, his listening ear, his healing, his food, his compassion, his patience, his wisdom, his encouragement. *He goes low and gives much.*

This is the brightness of God—the divine luminescence that

speaks. *Humility and giving*, the antithesis of selfishness and taking. Those are the things that darken our world.

Miller offered a portrait of this that fits perfectly with the theme of this book.

> God has called his human children to form a great circle where we all stand, arms linked together, facing toward the light in the center, which is God himself. We should see our fellow creatures standing around that central love that shines on us and illuminates our faces, and join with them in the dance of God, the rhythm of love. But instead of choosing to face the center, we have turned our backs on God and each other, and face the other way so that we can neither see the light at the center nor the faces in the circle. Instead of enjoying God and each other, we play our own selfish little game, each one wanting to be the center. No longer do we understand God or ourselves. The light of God still shines from the true center upon our backs, though not on our faces. Because we were created for something better, we are dimly aware that all is not well. We don't feel our separation from God but we feel its effects—a sense of deadness, of alienation, of profound loneliness, of cosmic emptiness.[117]

Even as we carry the Christ-light, we turn our backs to the God of light, holding our little candle in our chest. But we'll never burn as brightly, we'll never love as deeply, until we turn and face the true center, the light who goes low and gives himself away. *His* way must become *our* way.

> In a circle stood the souls of men,
> Ringing a light that glows and gives.
> Our faces warmed; a soft amen
> Went out to the God who lives.

> But we turned shoulders, showing backs.
> The light we held went dark and bleak.
> We wanted what we thought we lacked—
> To be the great light others seek.
> Yet the glowing, giving God pursued,
> To turn our shoulders back around.
> He sent himself to our great feud,
> Fit his feet for sandals, dropped a crown.
> His giving of his blood and bone
> Put God's own light inside of us.
> For there is one light, one love and throne
> That we encircle with our trust.
> Dark to light now, death to life,
> We go low and give back the light
> To other souls with wanting rife,
> Ready to lean out of the night.

But how do we actually give ourselves? This all sounds nice and poetic, but the poetic truth of God doesn't just warm our hearts; it *changes* us. It reshapes us, one tiny decision at a time. We can break these into two categories: decisions of humility and decisions of giving.

DECISIONS OF HUMILITY

Decisions of humility are those moments when we can see ourselves as higher than others, more deserving, more qualified, more experienced, more ambitious, more focused, more mature. Every "more" is laced with pride—even when we're sure we're right. But Jesus had not just the "more" in every category, but the "most." He is literally described as "all in all" (Col. 3:11). He's the highest, the best, the brightest . . . in *everything*. And yet we *never* read of him elevating himself above someone else. He rebuked the Pharisees, of course, but that was a matter of divine judgment. He never went into a temple during a lecture and said, "Hey, what do you think you're doing? Those scrolls are all about *me*. Let me do the teaching. You just sit down and be quiet." He never elevated himself; he only emptied himself. He had everything and yet came to lead and teach as a *servant*. He gave up every opportunity to silence others by the good reason of his divine identity. Even on the cross, when people wagged their heads at him and mocked, he never said, "Oh, you just wait! In three days, I'll show you just how ignorant and foolish you are!" He asks instead for his Father to forgive them (Luke 23:34). Why? Why on earth would he do that?

Because Jesus is the most faithful, consistent, dependable man in history. His principle of love was to go low and give much, just as his Father (John 3:16). That's what he did everyday. The cross was the boldest, most glorious demonstration of who Jesus always was . . . and is.

As his followers, we shouldn't be grasping at every chance to elevate ourselves, to show that *we're* the best choice, the most hard-working, the most deserving of promotion, respect, and accolades. When we do this, we go high and take much. And we can feel our soul diminish, precisely because that is not God's way.

Paul Miller wrote two short sentences that capture the thing at stake in all of our little decisions each day. "Jesus chose the lower place. That's what love does."[118] Love goes down, beneath, where the feet are. As the world screams for you and I to rise up, Jesus whispers, "Go low." Why? Because that's where he is. Down is where we go if we want to see people as Jesus did. As Miller put it,

> When we take the low place, we see clearly. Pride doesn't even notice humility, because humility is so quiet. But down low, you see not only other people better, but also yourself—and God—better. That's why the outcasts of society—children, women, foreigners, the poor and disabled—are attracted to Jesus. They see him clearly. They know they have nothing to put on the table; they are empty. Drawn by his beauty, they cling to his

love.[119]

We see God and others well when we are low because "God lives there."[120]

We have a plethora of moments each day to go low. Here's a recent example.

One of my children asked for a snack before bed, as is typical. I was tired and hoping to get to bed early.

"Come and get it in the kitchen," I said.

"Can you cut me up an apple?" came the voice from down the hallway. I sighed.

"Yea—hold on." I walked to the kitchen frustrated at first, but I made myself feel better by telling myself I was a servant. I can laugh at my own audacity. Jesus went to the cross to save souls; I'm going to the kitchen to cut an apple. Not quite the same level. But I don't let this thought deflate my ego too much. I still think I'm being pretty Christ-like. I am a servant apple preparer (just like Jesus?).

"Can you make sure it's cut into small pieces? Not the big ones you usually do?"

I really fought the urge to say, "Anything else, my lord? Shall I put it on our finest silver and then fetch a pillow for your feet?" But that wouldn't have helped anything. More to the point, it would have been trying to go high when I should be going low. Going high would sound like this internal discourse: "Hey, you're not a butler. These kids can get their own snack. You have more important things to do right now than cut up an apple . . . like sleep. Plus, it's enabling."

The ego can throw a hundred reasons ahead of itself to make you think you're acting out of someone else's best interest. I knew that wasn't the case. I didn't *want* to serve in this moment, not in *this* way.

But something told me that this is precisely when going low is tested. It was like I was saying, "Alright—I'll go low and serve. I'll get the kid an apple, even cut it. But I'm not custom-cutting this fruit. I'm not going *that* low."

Can you imagine Jesus taking that mentality? "Alright, Father. I'll get them a water basin and a towel for their feet, but I'm not scrubbing the mud off their nasty toes. That's where I draw the line." He'd *never* say something like that. First, because this suggests Jesus's will is against that of his Father, and there is only one will in God. But second, Jesus would never put limits on his servanthood this way. If he was going to draw a line, that would've happened *before* the whole incarnation, self-emptying business. He came an infinite distance from glory just to be here. All the lines were already crossed.

And so I sliced the apple into thin, easily-chewable mouthfuls and brought the bowl to my child. Most parents have to choose (or not choose) to do this sort of thing everyday. There are a thousand ways for parents to go low each day for their kids. Our ego just nags us to take a different path—preferably one that avoids apple-cutting and foot-washing.

Decisions of humility say, "Sure, I can serve." Or, "Go ahead; I want to hear what you have to say." Or, "I hadn't thought of it that way." Or—and here's the hardest—*nothing*. Silence is the hardest thing to say. But often it's the way of humility. Silence simply makes a way for others. Jesus made a way for us, and he was silent, like a sheep before its shearers (Isa. 53:7). If the Son of God walked the path of silence for our salvation, why are we so convinced that our speech would save a situation? We need to relearn the quiet beauty of silence. It's the unnoticed act that pushes others up while we go low.

Decisions of Giving

Deciding to go low is only half the battle. We also have to give something of ourselves to others. That's how Scripture seems to define love: self-giving. "For God so *loved* the world that he *gave*" (John 3:16). Giving can work itself out in lots of little actions, all of which are evident in Jesus's life. Jesus gave his . . .

- Time

- Teaching
- Listening ear
- Food
- Touch
- Emotions
- Encouragement
- Prayer
- Guidance
- Joy
- Lament
- Sympathy

He even gave fishing advice (Luke 5:4–6). There are many items on this list for us to choose from each day. The hard part is sensing when it's appropriate to give a certain thing. But if we're watching and listening, we'll be guided. A friend who bombs a job interview probably isn't looking for immediate feedback. He or she likely just wants you to listen—and maybe ask a good question or two.

Still the hardest part about giving ourselves to others is that the very act makes us vulnerable. What if they don't want what we have to give? What if they reject us? What if we open up a painful part of our past, and it just gets kicked to the curb?

I'm afraid vulnerability is part of love's package. In his book *The Four Loves*, C. S. Lewis wrote,

> To love at all is to be vulnerable. Love anything and your heart will be wrung and possibly bro-

ken. If you want to be sure of keeping it intact, you must give your heart to no one, not even an animal. Wrap it carefully round with hobbies and little luxuries; avoid all entanglements; lock it up safe in the casket or coffin of your selfishness. But in that casket—safe, dark, motionless, airless—it will change. It will not be broken; it will become unbreakable, impenetrable, irredeemable. . . . The only place outside of Heaven where you can be perfectly safe from all the dangers and perturbations of love is hell.[121]

Here on earth, we love and open ourselves to the dangers. To refuse to do so would be to reject Christ, whose love and vulnerability took him to the cross . . . but also to the dark of a tomb and then the brilliant light of resurrection. His resurrection life honors our little acts of giving each day. There is light ahead.

Go low and give much, my friends. That is the way of God. And so it must be *our* way.

REFLECT

1. What are the things that keep you from going low before others? Think of a specific example.

2. What are the things that you find you *want* to give to others? Do others sometimes want you to give something else?

3. "Silence is the hardest thing to say." When is it most difficult for you to be silent so that others can be lifted up?

PRAY

God of glory,
Who would guess that you—
The strongest and brightest—
Would go low to give much?
And yet you did.
You went the lowest
And you gave the most.
Your love is our salvation.
Your coming down means our going up.
Your emptying led to our filling.
Help us to follow you,
To find you in the low places,
So that we see the world aright.
And in that low place,
Show us what you want us to give.

CONCLUSION

CHRIST PUT HIS LIGHT in others. He put *himself* in others. He looked before he listened, and listened before he worked. He went to the darkest and made them the brightest. We need more practice at seeing his light.

As I've said in earlier chapters, we choose what we see. So often I'm prone to seeing the worst in others, which is probably a reflection of my own self-doubt. Seeing the worst in yourself primes you to see the worst in others. We need to start staring at the candles of Christ.

On Christmas Eve night each year, I wait in the sanctuary of the church for the lights to dim as each person grabs a candle and lights it with the wick of the one next to him. Before "O Holy Night" begins, we're all huddled together in the warm dark with our amber, swaying flames, small as fingertips.

It's just dawned on me that this moment is the church; it's all of us, standing in the world with our God-given candle—our relationship-bound, communion-loving, ever-reacting light of Christ. That's the light that God never takes his eyes off of, because that's the light of himself.

We are the candle kids, the flame-holders, the bearers of God's illumination. What we have inside us—it means everything. It's how God sees us, how he calls us to himself, how he loves us and how we love others. We are the candle kids.

Every morning we wake is an exercise in light-seeking, in staring at the aura God put in every redeemed heart, including our own. And the more frequently and deeply we stare at that light, the more we go low and give much, the brighter our souls will become.

Long live the God of day! Long live the Lord of light. As God sees us, may we see each other.

APPENDIX 1
How We See NonChristians

I'VE WRITTEN THIS BOOK for Christians. And early on I had to make the distinction between those whom God foreknew (Rom. 8:29) to be his children in Christ, and those whom he would create in his image and yet who wouldn't believe in him. How does seeing the light in fellow believers matter for how we interact with nonChristians? What's the main difference?

With Christians, seeing the Christ-light in them is an act of persevering encouragement and confidence. We see the light in them and act in the Spirit of Christ to brighten it because *that's their destiny*. Christians *are* children of light—housing the persons of the Godhead, filled with resurrection life and hope, carrying the will, heart, and work of God. They need to be prodded to own their God-given, grace-bestowed identity in a world that longs for restoration. The light we see in Christians is brightened by the Spirit's ongoing work of sanctification. Our prayer should be to encourage brothers and sisters with confidence in what God has already done in their hearts and in the great things he is about to do.

With nonChristians, however, it's different. While they are still image bearers of God and are responsible for believing in him and imitating him faithfully (covenant, communion, reaction), they have not yet opened themselves to the light of the world (John 8:12), the true light (John 1:5). And because of that, we're limited in what good things we can see in them. They have chosen to remain in the domain of darkness, and we can't see much in the dark. All we can see are the bits of light that fall on them from God's common grace.

We do know with certainty that they have a relationship with God (covenant), that they long to be with him (communion), and that they're always reacting to a world that everywhere reveals him. So, we can still ask the same sorts of questions we might ask Christians, but the answers would be wildly different. *Are you faithful? Do you love God? Do you hear God?* There is a hard "no" for each of these questions, and not the sort of "no" that means the Spirit is progressively making them more like Christ. It's a "no" that refuses the light of God, that *wills* to stay in darkness. They need Christ's faithfulness, love, and obedience in order to have a restored relationship with God. In that sense, our call is to draw such people to the beauty and forgiveness of Christ himself, praying that God might open their hearts to believe in his Son.

In that sense, we might ask a different set of questions when it comes to non-Christians.

- Where is there a longing for relational faithfulness that can't be met apart from Christ?

- What substitutes does the person have for communion with God, and what are the effects of these substitutes?

- What elements of God's revelation are being ignored or combatted, and why?

These questions may help us see what is holding the person back from believing in Christ, and how lasting fulfillment and purpose will be absent until that person's heart is moved by the Spirit to embrace the Christ-light.

Why am I saying all of this? Because while we all bear God's image as humans, that doesn't mean we'll interact with everyone in the exact same way, with the same assumptions and goals. Christians have had their doused and fuming wicks lit by Christ. They don't just know God and long for him; they *have* God hidden in their hearts and enjoy his presence each day. Because of God's presence, Christians are able to live a life of Christ-conformity by the Spirit. That's not something nonChristians can do. And because of that, we shouldn't suggest that nonChristians can "shine" as brightly as Christians.

I know it's unpopular to say that one human being burns brighter than another—that not all people burn with the same glow. But we have to say that in order to acknowledge the necessity of Christ's work. What Christ did *changed* things; he changed *us*. That distinction has to hold. No matter how much we might be tempted to say, "Well, we all have the same brightness before God," or "we're all God's children," we have to stare at the truth of God's word and affirm that apart from the Spirit of Christ, it's not even possible to please God (Rom. 8:8).

I say this not to encourage a sort of pride in Christians but to emphasize the missional task of the church. Many people *need* the light of Christ. They won't skate merrily through life without him. They won't see themselves or the world rightly apart from his life-giving light. They need the great Chandler to light their wick. And it's our task to point to that Chandler with our words and actions.

We can't force anyone to believe in Christ, but we can and must claim that apart from him, no one will ever burn eternally with God in love and peace. And here on earth, our wicks are black and fuming unless Christ enters the heart chamber. Burning brightly isn't a matter of trying harder, some sort of stark moralism that's void of grace. That would leave God out of the picture and suggest that we can all burn brighter if we just make the extra effort. God is at the center. He *is* the light. It is only through him and in him that we'll be our truest selves and illumine others around us.

To put it shortly, seeing the light in Christians is a matter of encouragement in the faith, while engaging with nonChristians is a missional and apologetic task, aimed at pointing them to the glow of the gospel.

APPENDIX 2

BARRIERS TO SEEING THE LIGHT IN BELIEVERS

WE KNOW THAT SEEING the light in other believers is no easy task. God can and will help us do this as we grow in him, but it's good at the outset to have a sense of the barriers to seeing the light in others. What blinds us? What obstacles get in the way that must be removed?

Ultimately, this is a question of what keeps us from *loving* other people. Mike Emlet discusses some practical reasons why we struggle to love other Christians in his book *Saints, Sufferers, and Sinners: Loving Others as God Loves Us*. I'll outline his list, adding one of my own at the start.

1. We're pessimists. I noted earlier that my own self-doubt pushes me to see only the worst in myself, but this has the added effect of pushing me to see the worst in others.[122] A pessimistic attitude looks for the darkness in every arena of life—a reason for doubt, distrust, discouragement, hopelessness, skepticism. Rather than looking for the Christ-light in others, my impulse is to look for and even assume the darkness. And yet I can't even number the times my assumptions about others have been dead wrong. Someone I think is haughty or self-righteous is actually trying to set out what God has been teaching him. Someone whom I think is being hyper-critical of me is actually trying to love me based on the mistakes she made in the past.

The most damaging effect of being a pessimist is that it downplays or utterly discards the redemptive work of God in someone else's life. It says, "Yea, I know you say you've been redeemed by the God of light, but I don't know; I see a lot of darkness." How audacious it is to claim knowledge of someone else's stance before God! Rather than doubting or downplaying God's work in someone else, I should believe in it and act on it. In fact, my belief in others' ongoing redemption may well end up being a boost of encouragement for them as they develop in their faith.

2. We forget that the "saint" category for a Christian is more primary than the "sinner" category.[123] This is related to the previous point. We know that we're all "saints and sinners"; we're all in process. And yet we assume that these labels are equally ultimate. But to do that is to doubt the work of God and look down on the sacrifice of Christ and the power of the Spirit. God himself has promised that he will complete his good, saintly work in the heart of every believer (Phil. 1:6). Do we really want to doubt the God of truth? If he's promised this, why do we focus so much on the sin in someone else rather than the redemption God is working? Why do we stare at the remnant darkness when the Christ-light is burning right in front of us?

We have a choice in what we see. Personally, this has taken practice in repeating the truth, "This person is brightening in the Spirit of Christ; Lord, you *are* working, regardless of whether or not I see it." The sainthood of another believer needs to stay in the foreground, while the indwelling sin remains in the background. To flip this around is to doubt the very word of God. It's a big deal.

3. We think we're better than other people.[124] This is a silent killer of communion and relationship. Rather than following in the footsteps of humility pressed into the earth by the Son of God, we pretend to walk a higher road. This can often be spotted in statements such as, "I can't believe she did that!" Or, "Why would he think that?" The assumption behind these statements is that *we* would never act in this way. We need a healthy dose of 1 Timothy 1:15. We are the worst. There's no one beneath us. We're not in *less* need of the redemptive work of the Spirit than someone else. We need to stop the comparison game. We need to stop measuring ourselves horizontally (in relation to others) and measure ourselves vertically (in relation to Christ). In relation to Christ, we need *a lot* of work. All of us. If we ever assume we're better than another believer—no matter how distant we feel we are from them in a particular sin—we're going to struggle to see the Christ-light in them. We're going to struggle to *love*. And since love is the mark of a Christian (John 13:35), that's critical. Put everyone above you. When you're on the bottom, that's where Christ is, too. You'll see things from a perspective of grace and forgiveness.

4. We're reactive rather than proactive in engaging others.[125] Emlet notes, "When we experience sin in others' lives, particularly if it's directed toward us, we tend to react out of our own hurt and discomfort, rather than proactively considering the call to love the other person well."[126] We're never at our best when we're reacting. Why? Because reacting isn't as intentional; it's instinctive, and our instincts need redeeming. Think about it physically. Are you better at catching a baseball when you ask someone to throw it to you or when someone throws it at you and then yells, "Hey, catch!" The latter is a reaction to something. It's not an intentional movement with your body. So, no one blames you for dropping the ball. But in the former scenario, you're proactive. You're intentionally calling for the ball, and so your body movements are measured and patient.

The same applies in the spiritual world. Before we even engage with another person, we have the proactive call from Christ: "Love one another" (John 13:34). That's where we *start* every conversation. Love is much harder to show reactively. But proactively, the Spirit can help us guard and direct our hearts. Seeing the Christ-light in others requires that we be proactive, and that we pray earnestly for the Spirit to teach us this.

5. "We struggle with fear of man and people-pleasing."[127] I really battle this on a daily basis. I'm a conflict avoider. In high-school, I was part of a peer-mediation group that helped students sort out conflicts peacefully. Sometimes the agreement between students would amount to, "Okay, well you take this hallway to your science class, and she'll take this other hallway to math. That way, you won't cross paths." I would stutter at this sort of resolution. "But, but, but they didn't solve the conflict!"

I responded this way because, as a people-pleaser, I can't stand when someone isn't happy with me. It eats away at me. This is tied to a fear of man. If I really cared primarily about what God thought of me, I wouldn't be so needy for the approval of others.

Many times we avoid engaging with others—especially when sin and hurt is involved—because we're afraid of causing more pain, of breaking the relationship, of having someone think less of us. And so we don't engage. We let things sit.

We need courage. And we need to remember that really loving other believers, really seeing the Christ-light in them, is a matter of holding fast to the truth—about who God is, who we are, and what our purpose is as followers of Christ. We can be sure that this *won't* please people. Truth doesn't let things lie where they are; it changes the world. That's what Christ did, and he *is* the truth (John 14:6).

6. It's easier not to see the Christ-light in others.[128] It takes more effort and intentionality to see Christ's light in other believers because we're all in process. But redemption is never easy. Do we think it was easy for Christ to walk into a hall of tax collectors and sinners? How many head-shakes did he get? How many eye-rolls? How many judging looks? How many times did people even think, "This guy belongs with them; he's a bastard child himself. His own mother is a prostitute." We shudder at those words, but Jesus faced *a lot* of adversity and pushback simply because of his birth narrative. It would have been easier for Jesus to stay in the common areas of the cities, keeping himself distant from the down-and-out crowds. But he did the hard thing. And he did it again, and again, and again. He went to give his light to others, but this took great effort, patience, intentionality, and courage. It may be harder to see the Christ-light in fellow believers, but if that's what *Christ* gave them, I want to see it, because I want to see *him*.

7. Our own shame and guilt cripple us.[129] Shame and guilt darken us. As with Adam and Eve in Genesis 3, shame and guilt encourage us to grab fig leaves and cover ourselves. We don't want anyone looking at us, and we certainly don't want to draw any attention to some sort of light inside us. When we're focused on covering ourselves, we don't see others so well. With our heads turned down, we can't notice the burning wick of another soul. This is a tough reality, since in Christian circles, shame and guilt are responses of repentance. They can show that we want to change. And that confuses people into thinking that shame and guilt are virtuous in some redemptive way. While that's certainly the case for people in specific situations, shame and guilt are *never* meant to be places where Christians live. We stop there for a time, but we don't stay. And if our shame and guilt is keeping us from seeing the light in God's people, that's a sign we've been staying too long. Our shame and guilt are covered in Christ. We put him on as a garment (Rom. 13:14). We don't have to be afraid of being seen. If other Christians' eyes are working properly, they'll see *him*—his grace, his patience, his mercy, his forgiveness. If they don't see that, maybe they need their eyes checked, or they're dealing with #3 above.

1. Remember that I am addressing Christians in this book. Romans 8:29 references Christian believers, whose doused wicks were lit in Christ, by the Spirit, according to the mysterious love of the Father.

2. John Murray, *The Epistle to the Romans: The English Text with Introduction, Exposition, and Notes* (Glenside, PA: Westminster Seminary Press, 2022), 489.

3. J. Gresham Machen, *Things Unseen: A Systematic Introduction to the Christian Faith and Reformed Theology* (Glenside, PA: Westminster Seminary Press, 2020), 9.

4. Cornelius Van Til, *Common Grace and the Gospel*, 2nd ed., ed. K. Scott Oliphint (Phillipsburg, NJ: P&R, 2015), 8–9).

5. Vern S. Poythress, "Introducing the Law of Christ (Lex Christi): A Fruitful Framework for Theology and Life," The Works of John Frame & Vern Poythress, https://frame-poythress.org/introducing-the-law-of-christ-lex-christi-a-fruitful- framework-for-theology-and-life/.

6. "You Are They: Human Identity and the Trinity," *Westminster Magazine*, https://wm.wts.edu/content/you-are-they- human-identity-and-the-trinity.

7. The short answers to these questions are "for his glory" and "because he loves us."

8. John Calvin, *Institutes of the Christian Religion: Translated from the First French Edition of 1541*, trans. Robert White (Carlisle, PA: Banner of Truth, 2014), 10.

9. Herman Bavinck, *God and Creation*, vol. 2 of *Reformed Dogmatics*, ed. John Bolt, trans. John Vriend (Grand Rapids, MI: Baker Academic, 2004), 186.

10. See chapter 5 in *Finding God in the Ordinary* (Eugene, OR: Wipf & Stock, 2018).

11. *The Great Lie: What All of Hell Wants You to Keep Believing* (Independently published, 2022).

12. We cannot gather all the meaning in Scripture on the image of God or reduce it to a simple list of traits. Saying, "To bear God's image means that we are _____" amounts to a reduction, often motivated by a desire to control things. Scripture is richer than we can fathom in its teaching on how we imitate God as image-bearers. And the call to explore all the ways in which we image God is simultaneously a call to live out those ways in application of the unified and yet diverse biblical teaching on the image of God and the light of Christ.

13. Bavinck, *God and Creation*, 252.

14. Bavinck, *God and Creation*, 253.

15. Rich Villodas, *Good and Beautiful and Kind: Becoming Whole in a Fractured World* (Colorado Springs, CO: Waterbrook, 2022), xx.

16. Robert Letham, *Systematic Theology* (Wheaton, IL: Crossway, 2019), 128.

17. John Murray, *The Epistle to the Romans: The English Text with Introduction, Exposition, and Notes* (Glenside, PA: Westminster Seminary Press, 2022), 306.

18. These lines come from his poem "Love II."

19. Bavinck, *God and Creation*, 254.

20. Bavinck, *God and Creation*, 254.

21. Joel Clarkson, *Sensing God: Experiencing the Divine Nature in Food, Music, and Beauty* (Colorado Springs, CO: NavPress, 2021), 26.

22. Clarkson, *Sensing God*, 26.

23. Note that this beauty is bound up with God's truth and love. We cannot neatly detach one attribute of God from another, since all of God's attributes are prismatic, refracting light onto every other attribute.

24. Mary Oliver, "Mysteries, Yes," in *Devotions: The Selected Poems of Mary Oliver* (New York: Penguin, 2017), 85.

25. Clarkson, *Sensing God*, 122.

26. Herman Bavinck, *The Wonderful Works of God: Instruction in the Christian Religion according to the Reformed Confession* (Glenside, PA: Westminster Seminary Press, 2019), 116.

27. John Frame notes "Good is the broadest possible term of approval." But he goes on to distinguish different kinds of goodness—a goodness of purpose (teleological), beauty (aesthetic), morality, etc. In short, "when God declared the creation good, he meant good in every sense appropriate to every creature." *Systematic Theology: An Introduction to Christian Belief* (Phillipsburg, NJ: P&R, 2013), 845.

28. Keep in mind that when we looked at light as a metaphor for who God is, we were looking through an element of creation that reflects its Creator, since "the light that God creates through his speech reflects on a creaturely level the God who is light (1 John 1:5)." Vern S. Poythress, *The Mystery of the Trinity: A Trinitarian Approach to the Attributes of God* (Phillipsburg, NJ: P&R, 2020), 492.

29. Vern S. Poythress, *In the Beginning Was the Word: Language—A God-Centered Approach* (Wheaton, IL: Crossway, 2009), 25.

30. Poythress refers to the Son of God as the "mediator of meaning." *The Mystery of the Trinity*, 539.

31. Vern S. Poythress, *Redeeming Philosophy: A God-Centered Approach to the Big Questions* (Wheaton, IL: Crossway, 2014), 23.

32. My discussion here relies on conversations with Vern Poythress as well as his manuscript *Biblical Teaching on Humanity*.

33. T. P. Yates develops the concept of lex Christi in his dissertation, "Adapting Westminster Standards' Moral Law Motif to Integrate Systematic Theology, Apologetics and Pastoral Practice," thesis, North-West University, 2021, https://bethoumyvision.net/wp-content/uploads/2022/12/TP-YATES-31568734-APOL-971-PhD-Thesis.pdf. I'm indebted to him as well, especially for understanding how we imitate God in these areas.

34. Vern S. Poythress, *Biblical Teaching on Humanity: Classical Theology with New Methods* (prepublication manuscript), 73–88.

35. In the Reformed tradition, people usually say that we image God in knowledge, righteousness, and holiness. I also argue in *The Speaking Trinity & His Worded World* that language is another important avenue for this imaging (we image God by communicating, as he communicates with himself). But in this book, I'm going even broader than that, in a way that I'm convinced captures more of the teaching of Scripture.

36. Cornelius Van Til, *Common Grace and the Gospel*, 2nd ed., ed. K. Scott Oliphint (Phillipsburg, NJ: P&R, 2015), 232.

37. John Murray, *The Epistle to the Romans: The English Text with Introduction, Exposition, and Notes* (Glenside, PA: Westminster Seminary Press, 2022), 56.

38. John Calvin, *Institutes of the Christian Religion: Translated from the First French Edition of 1541*, trans. Robert White (Carlisle, PA: Banner of Truth, 2014), 3–4.

39. K. Scott Oliphint, *Covenantal Apologetics: Principles & Practice in Defense of Our Faith* (Wheaton, IL: Crossway, 2013), 13.

40. Geerhardus Vos, *Reformed Dogmatics: A System of Christian Theology*, ed. and trans. Richard B. Gaffin Jr. (Bellingham, WA: Lexham, 2020), 231–232.

41. From his poem "Man."

42. Kelly M. Kapic, *You're Only Human: How Your Limits Reflect God's Design and Why That's Good News* (Grand Rapids, MI: Brazos, 2022), 151.

43. Cornelius Van Til, *Common Grace and the Gospel*, 2nd ed., ed. K. Scott Oliphint (Phillipsburg, NJ: P&R, 2015), 237.

44. Van Til, *Common Grace and the Gospel*, 238.

45. Murray, *The Epistle to the Romans*, 56.

46. Rankin Wilbourne, *Union with Christ: The Way to Know and Enjoy God* (East Sussex, England: David C Cook, 2016), 15, Kindle edition.

47. Murray, *The Epistle to the Romans*, 489.

48. Murray, *The Epistle to the Romans*, 57.

49. Murray, *The Epistle to the Romans*, 57.

50. Dallas Willard, *Hearing God: Developing a Conversational Relationship with God*, updated and expanded ed. (Downers Grove, IL: IVP Books, 2012), 201.

51. Three persons, actually. See John 14:23; Rom. 8:11.

52. Willard, *Hearing God*, 190.

53. Willard, *Hearing God*, 190.

54. Willard, *Hearing God*, 194–195.

55. Willard, *Hearing God*, 203.

56. Willard, *Hearing God*, 210.

57. Murray, *The Epistle to the Romans*, 294.

58. Kapic, *You're Only Human*, 11.

59. Kapic, *You're Only Human*, 13.

60. Kapic, *You're Only Human*, 53.

61. Charlie Mackesy, *The Boy, the Mole, the Fox and the Horse* (New York: HarperOne, 2019),

62. Herman Bavinck, *God and Creation*, vol. 2 of *Reformed Dogmatics*, ed. John Bolt, trans. John Vriend (Grand Rapids, MI: Baker Academic, 2004), 191–192.

63. Geerhardus Vos, *The Eschatology of the Old Testament*, ed. James T. Dennison Jr. (Phillipsburg, NJ: P&R, 2001), 73.

64. Geerhardus Vos, *Reformed Dogmatics: A System of Christian Theology*, ed. and trans. Richard B. Gaffin Jr. (Bellingham, WA: Lexham, 2020), 176.

65. See Pierce Taylor Hibbs, *The Trinity, Language, and Human Behavior: A Reformed Exposition of the Language Theory of Kenneth L. Pike*, Reformed Academic Dissertations (Phillipsburg, NJ: P&R, 2018). See also

66. Paul E. Miller, *Love Walked among Us: Learning to Love Like Jesus* (Colorado Springs, CO: NavPress, 2014), 200.

67. John Calvin, *Institutes of the Christian Religion: Translated from the First French Edition of 1541*, trans. Robert White (Carlisle, PA: Banner of Truth, 2014), 207.

68. David Whyte, *Consolations: The Solace, Nourishment and Underlying Meaning of Everyday Words* (Langley, WA: Many Rivers, 2018), 19.

69. Whyte, *Consolations*, 19.

70. "Eating with Sinners: Why Jesus Broke the 'Rules,'" Olive Tree Blog, https://www.olivetree.com/blog/eating-with-sinners-why-jesus-broke-the-rules/.

71. Herman Bavinck, *God and Creation*, vol. 2 of *Reformed Dogmatics*, ed. John Bolt, trans. John Vriend (Grand Rapids, MI: Baker Academic, 2004), 216.

72. Vern S. Poythress, *The Mystery of the Trinity: A Trinitarian Approach to the Attributes of God* (Phillipsburg, NJ: P&R, 2020), 566.

73. Herman Bavinck, *Sin and Salvation in Christ*, vol. 3 of *Reformed Dogmatics*, ed. John Bolt, trans. John Vriend (Grand Rapids, MI: Baker Academic, 2006), 498.

74. Paul E. Miller, *Love Walked among Us: Learning to Love Like Jesus* (Colorado Springs, CO: NavPress, 2014), 31.

75. Miller, *Love Walked among Us*, 33.

76. Bavinck, *Sin and Salvation in Christ*, 279.

77. John Murray, *The Epistle to the Romans: The English Text with Introduction, Exposition, and Notes* (Glenside, PA: Westminster Seminary Press, 2022), 288.

78. This doesn't at all mean that doctrine isn't important. It's hugely important! But doctrine is not what Jesus identifies as the primary mark of his followers.

79. Adam S. McHugh, *The Listening Life: Embracing Attentiveness in a World of Distraction* (Downers Grove, IL: InterVarsity, 2015), 18.

80. David Whyte, *Consolations: The Solace, Nourishment and Underlying Meaning of Everyday Words* (Langley, WA: Many Rivers, 2018), 33.

81. Geerhardus Vos, "Hebrews, The Epistle of the Diatheke," in *Redemptive History and Biblical Interpretation: The Shorter Writings of Geerhardus Vos*, ed. Richard B. Gaffin Jr. (Phillipsburg, NJ: P&R, 1980), 186.

82. McHugh, *The Listening Life*, 43.

83. McHugh, *The Listening Life*, 44.

84. McHugh, *The Listening Life*, 144–145.

85. McHugh, *The Listening Life*, 145.

86. McHugh, *The Listening Life*, 144–145.

87. Craig Blomberg, "Introduction to the Parables," The Gospel Coalition, https://www.thegospelcoalition.org/essay/introduction-to-the-parables/.

88. Blomberg, "Introduction to the Parables."

89. Vern S. Poythress, *God-Centered Biblical Interpretation* (Phillipsburg, NJ: P&R, 1999), 183.

90. Poythress, *God-Centered Biblical Interpretation*, 174–175.

91. Kenneth L. Pike, *With Heart and Mind: A Personal Synthesis of Scholarship and Devotion* (Grand Rapids, MI: William B. Eerdmans, 1962), 75.

92. Pike, *With Heart and Mind*, 73.

93. Tim Keller, *Forgive: Why Should I and How Can I?* (New York: Viking, 2022), 6.

94. Keller, *Forgive*, 6.

95. Dallas Willard, *Hearing God: Developing a Conversational Relationship with God*, updated and expanded ed. (Downers Grove, IL: IVP, 2012), 134.

96. Willard, *Hearing God*, 134.

97. Keller, *Forgive*, 10.

98. Keller, *Forgive*, 164.

99. John Murray, *The Epistle to the Romans: The English Text with Introduction, Explanation, and Notes* (Glenside, PA: Westminster Seminary Press, 2022), 113.

100. Cornelius Van Til, *Common Grace and the Gospel*, 2nd ed., ed. K. Scott Oliphint (Phillipsburg, NJ: P&R, 2015), 237.

101. I wrote about this in the context of Fyodor Dostoevsky's *The Brothers Karamazov* here: "Dostoevsky and the Panacea for Personal Judgement," Reformed Journal, June 30, 2017, https://reformedjournal.com/dostoevsky-panacea-personal-judgment/.

102. Fyodor Dostoevsky, *The Brothers Karamazov*, Everyman's Library 70, trans. Richard Pevear and Larissa Volokhonsky (New York: Alfred A. Knopf, 1992), 320–321.

103. Dostoevsky, *The Brothers Karamazov*, 164.

104. Thomas Merton, *New Seeds of Contemplation* (Boston: Shambhala, 1961), 94–95.

105. Rich Villodas, *Good and Beautiful and Kind: Becoming Whole in a Fractured World* (Colorado Springs, CO: Waterbrook, 2022), 9.

106. Villodas, *Good and Beautiful and Kind*, 3.

107. Geerhardus Vos, *Reformed Dogmatics: A System of Christian Theology*, ed. and trans. Richard B. Gaffin Jr. (Bellingham, WA: Lexham, 2020), 261–262.

108. John M. Frame, *The Doctrine of the Knowledge of God*, A Theology of Lordship (Phillipsburg, NJ: P&R, 1987), 13.

109. Annie Dillard, *Pilgrim at Tinker Creek*, HarperPerennial Modern Classics (New York: HarperCollins, 1999), 223–224.

110. Dallas Willard, *Hearing God: Developing a Conversational Relationship with God*, updated and expanded ed. (Downers Grove, IL: IVP, 2012), 282–283.

111. John Murray, *The Epistle to the Romans: The English Text with Introduction, Exposition, and Notes* (Glenside, PA: Westminster Seminary Press, 2022), 438.

112. Willard, *Hearing God*, 135–136.

113. I have found John Mark Comer's work very helpful here: *Live No Lies: Recognize and Resist the Three Enemies That Sabotage Your Peace* (Colorado Springs, CO: Waterbook, 2021).

114. Paul E. Miller, *Loved Walked among Us: Learning to Love Like Jesus* (Carol Stream, IL: NavPress, 2014), 193.

115. Miller, *Loved Walked among Us*, 194.

116. Miller, *Love Walked among Us*, 194.

117. Miller, *Love Walked among Us*, 198.

118. Miller, *Love Walked among Us*, 211.

119. Miller, *Love Walked among Us*, 213.

120. Miller, *Love Walked among Us*, 214.

121. C. S. Lewis, *The Four Loves* (New York: HarperCollins, 1960), chap. 6. Kindle edition.

122. I talk about this openly in *Finding Hope in Hard Things: A Positive Take on Suffering*.

123. Michael R. Emlet, *Saints, Sufferers, and Sinners: Loving Others as God Loves Us* (Greensboro, NC: New Growth, 2021), 160–161.

124. "We exhibit self-righteousness and a judgmental spirit in our approach, negating the impact of our words." Emlet, *Saints, Sufferers, and Sinners*, 161.

125. Emlet, *Saints, Sufferers, and Sinners*, 161–162.

126. Emlet, *Saints, Sufferers, and Sinners*, 161–162.

127. Emlet, *Saints, Sufferers, and Sinners*, 162.

128. "We are motivated by laziness, comfort, or the status quo." Emlet, *Saints, Sufferers, and Sinners*, 163.

129. Emlet, *Saints, Sufferers, and Sinners*, 163.

About the Author

Pierce Taylor Hibbs (MAR, ThM Westminster Theological Seminary) is an award-winning Christian wordsmith and educator who builds things to bring readers closer to God. He's the author of over 15 books, including *Theological English* (2019 ECPA Finalist), *Finding God in the Ordinary*, *The Speaking Trinity & His Worded World*, *Struck Down but Not Destroyed* (Bronze Medalist in the 2021 Illumination Book Awards), *Finding Hope in Hard Things*, *The Book of Giving* (Gold Medalist in the 2022 Illumination Book Awards), and *The Great Lie* (Bronze Medalist in the 2023 Illumination Book Awards). He serves as Senior Writer and Communication Specialist at Westminster Theological Seminary. He and his wife, Christina, reside in Pennsylvania with their three kids. Download a free ebook and other resources from piercetaylorhibbs.com.

Leave a Review!

One the biggest ways you can bless an author is simply by leaving a concise, honest review of the book on a site such as Amazon, GoodReads, or Barnes & Noble. It takes very little time, but it makes a big difference in helping other readers find the book and give it a chance. If this book has helped you in your walk with the Lord, please consider leaving a brief, candid review. Thank you!

www.ingramcontent.com/pod-product-compliance
Lightning Source LLC
LaVergne TN
LVHW041949070526
838199LV00051BA/2964